Freedom at the Fair

Adam Blue

Copyright © Adam Blue 2019

adamablue.com

All rights reserved. No part of this book can be reproduced in any form without the written permission of the publisher, except in the case of brief quotations embodied in critical articles or reviews.

Stone House Press
247 Burr Road
Cornish, NH 03745

First Printing, 2019

ISBN: 9781798905975

This book is lovingly dedicated
to my family.

The fair is a jewel in summer's crown. It's an annual ritual in rural America—an institution rooted in our agricultural past that has transcended its origins to become something greater. The fair is that rare special occasion where you can escape the everyday and feel free. Free to explore. Free to wonder. Free to laugh. Free to play. Free to be.

At every turn, the fair is sweet. But it can be salty, too. It's a weekend you look forward to all year, peppered with surprises you would never dream up. It's adrenaline, sore feet, and sunburn. And just when you catch your breath, it's gone.

I love the fair. I always have.

☞ 👍 ☞

Where I grew up in California, the county fair was one long weekend in early July. Everything changed in that short time. A vacant lot became a site for magic. The skyline transformed, sprouting colorful new geometries. FM radio ads teased us, announcing the bands that were scheduled to play. The sun felt hotter. Smiles grew bigger. Everybody shined.

As junior high students, we made elaborate plans to see the fair as a group. And our parents would let us, assuming there was safety in numbers. I remember how we darted through the exhibitions and breezed between the vendors. How we swam through swarms of strangers. Endless temptations flashed before us as we approached the midway: candies, prizes, rides. Pausing, we would dare each other to flirt with cliques from other schools. Go talk to them, they're so beautiful. Then we'd blend back into the crowd, laughing. In the playful randomness we could be bolder, different, more. But we also had to be vigilant. The high school kids could fuck you up. They were clever, cruel, and sticky with b.o. They had heavy metal t-shirts, roach clips, and unpredictable ways. If you got caught, your ass was grass.

And, of course, there were the carneys. Barkers calling from every direction. Your ears perked as your feet slowed. Eye contact with a carney was like a tractor beam. "Come here," they'd say as they waved you in. "Try your luck. It's only one dollar."

The games at the fair are like riddles in old storybooks. Double talk, simple rules, and the promise of a bounty beyond imagination. You were too old for stuffed animals, but damn it's twice your height. Worse, the games taunted you. It's just an ordinary dart, a baseball, a plastic ring, a water gun, a machine gun, a balloon. Were the rules stacked against you? Obviously. Everything is rigged. But you could totally do it.

"Let me demonstrate." By then it was too late. The carney had you on the hook. "What's your name, kid?"

"Larry," you lied, heart pounding. You'd wear a straight face to try and impress your friends. But still you walked closer.

The carneys came from a different world and lived by a different code. They didn't care if you sassed them. They'd clap back, their cigarette-roughened voices calling from the tinny speakers behind the prizes. They recognized your teenage attitude and upped the stakes, conjuring a crowd behind you with a well timed barb. Oof. Now everyone else was watching you, too. The carneys gave you control, but you were always a mark. It was never a fair match.

I remember the midway rides as beautiful mayhem. Bright colors, flashing lights, hissing sounds and screams. Risk and reward. Terror and pleasure.

The rides for the little kids featured trucks and rocket ships. The fiberglass vehicles spun in tight circles with the occasional jolt up or down. Some parents folded themselves into the seats, accompanying their toddlers through waves of dizziness. Other parents leaned across the metal fence, cameras recording. We had outgrown this section of the fair. We were cooler than it, except for the nostalgia. We moved on.

Puberty pits everyone against the measuring pole. You must be at least this tall to enjoy this ride. Strategies emerged: straightened spines, uncombed hair, gym shoes that add an inch. You made it.

The scariest rides became rites of passage. Every successive summer opened more extreme delights. Tea Cups last year, Scrambler this, the Zipper maybe if the worker wasn't paying attention. I remember arching my back to pass the ruler, then getting on to realize the packed-out safety pads wouldn't hold me in the ride. What the fuck have you done—a kid last year fell out and died on this one. The screams came from a different place. Blood rushed sideways and knuckles turned white. The sky, it's beneath your feet. Holy shit, holy shit, holy shit. That was way too short. I'm not sure I feel so good. Hold on. Should we do it again? Do you want to try a different one?

Our crew headed to a gentler ride to recover. The group dynamic shifted once again, young hearts still racing. I dare you to ride this with him or her. Go ask. Would you go on this one with me? You'd never admit it, but you hoped your bodies would be thrown together, touching in unusual ways. Well, okay. Look around to see who's seeing you together. Let's. Then the extended waits. A surge of action. False start. More people loading. Anxious jokes in the air between you. Finally it begins and the smiles are true.

Decades later, fully grown, and a parent now letting my kids run free, I still love the freedoms of the fair. But in completely different ways.

The photographs in this book were taken between 2006 and 2018 at fairs in Western Massachusetts, Vermont, and New Hampshire. The pride of place in rural New England is profound. Which is as it should be. The magic of the fair, though, is that regardless of location, the fair reflects and informs its community's will to perfection.

The spirit of rural New England fairs is more closely tied to agriculture than those I grew up with in California. The celebrations here showcase our next generation of farmers as they exhibit their prized cows, sheep, chickens, rabbits, pigs, and horses—to name a few. The bond between the children and the animals is clear. You can see it in the responsibilities the kids gracefully manage: trailering in, trailering out, watering, washing, feeding, walking, tending, brushing, grooming, mucking. By late afternoon, their white show clothes are stained at the knees and cuffs. And their pockets overflow with ribbons. It's pretty wonderful.

The gardening competitions are like a quiet, knowing nod. Giant pumpkins, perfect tomatoes, corn twice your height. It's not flashy. The fruits and vegetables filling the tables speak to a different kind of caring. Planting, pruning, weeding. The cycle of the seasons. The local bounty manifest. Back in the city, they'd label this exhibit "farm-to-table" and double the entry price.

Next door there are the pies, cakes, canned jams and jellies. The wisdom folded into these family recipes weaves generations together. More than confections, these treats are the cultural currency of appreciation. Gifting and trading pies or jams isn't like exchanging money in the countryside. They're offered and received with modest pride. Add a blue ribbon to the mix, your neighbors will know without being told.

Speaking of sweets, the food at the fair has jettisoned all dietary restraint. Portions are doubled. Deep fryers work triple time. Salt and sugar are tossed like confetti. It's heaven, if only for a day.

The arts and crafts at the fair are gorgeous. Participants of all ages and abilities create their submissions with honest intentions. The materials are usually modest. The ideas are always playful. If you attend the fairs regularly, you'll see the same people entering works year after year. Each piece is a touchstone in their understanding of what art is and can be. In slow motion, you can see voices evolving over time.

And then there are the tractors. The oxen. The horses. The woodsman games. The motors, hooves, axes, and saws inspire exhibitions of speed, strength, and accuracy. These competitions are real crowd-pleasers. The bleachers fill to capacity quickly, so people bring folding chairs to stay throughout the day. There's an adult energy in the arena, a seriousness not found on the midway. A lifetime of hard work, skill, and concentration are being put on display. Trophies, cash prizes, and a year of bragging rights are on the line. But beneath the bravado of the souped-up machines and the sharp cutting edges, you can tell that the participants' inner children have come to play. There's freedom at the fair for these serious competitors, too. It's a freedom from the daily grind, when all the same gestures are done in service to work.

☞ ☝ ☞

So step right up. And try your luck. There's a winner every time.

I hope you enjoy the show.

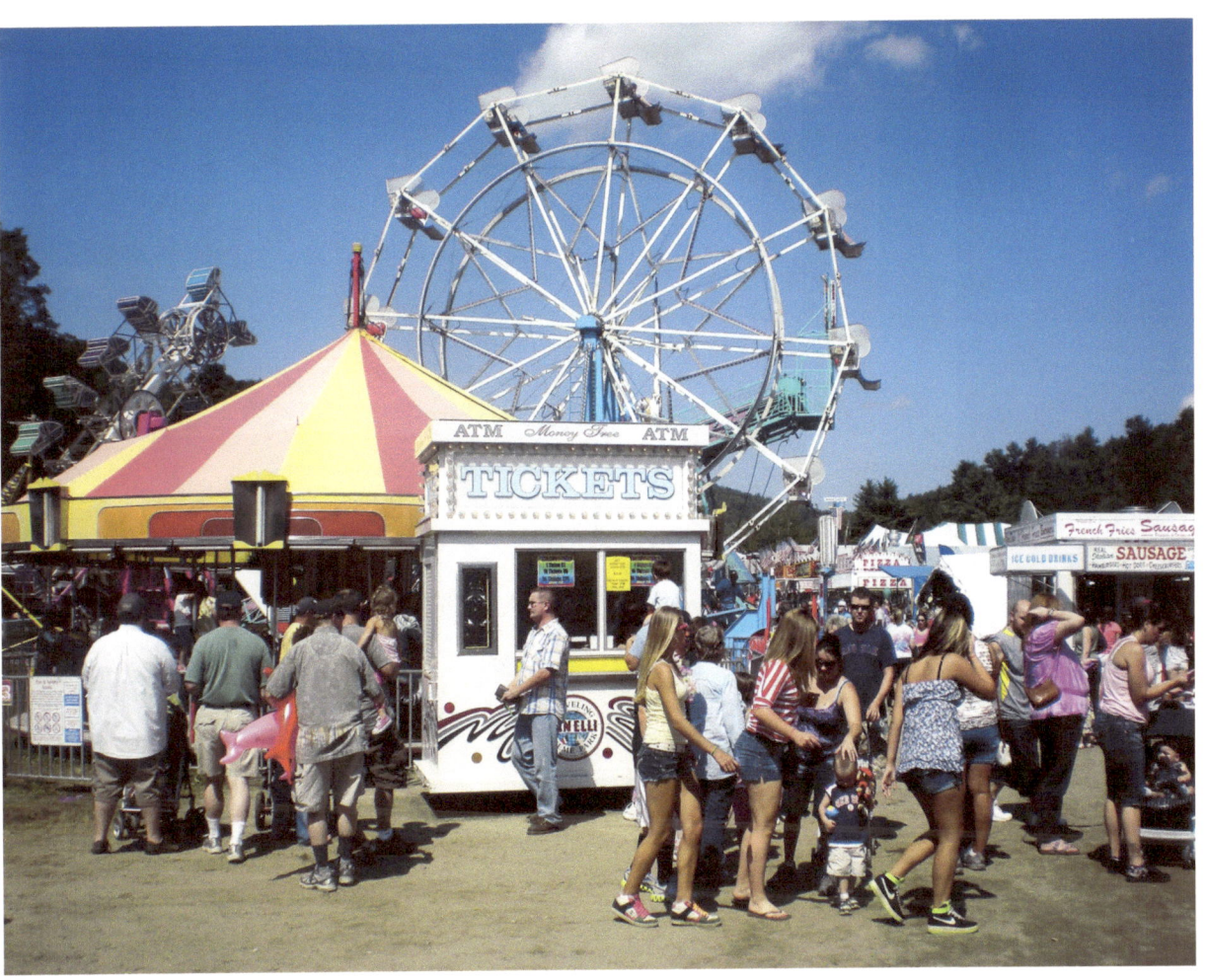

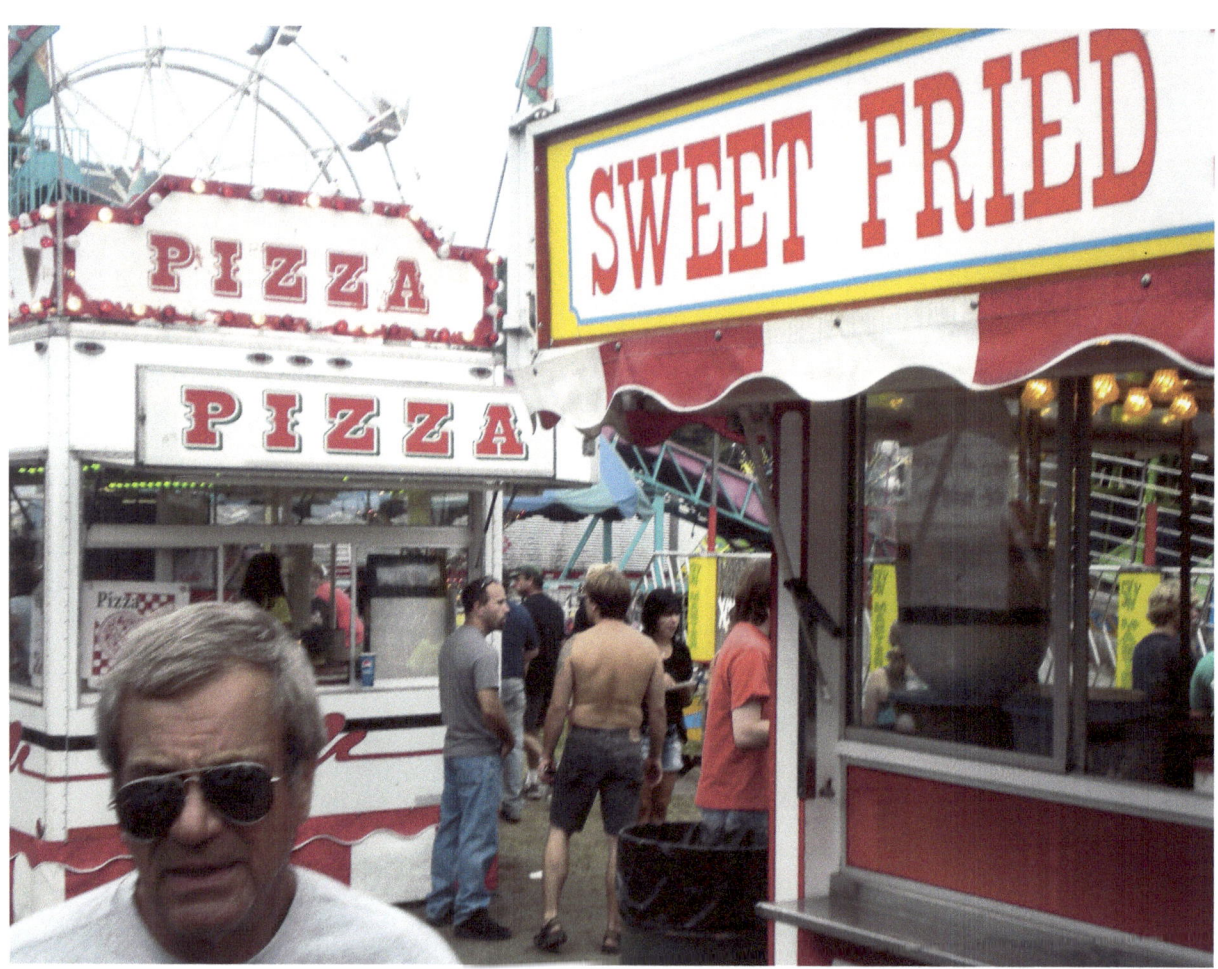

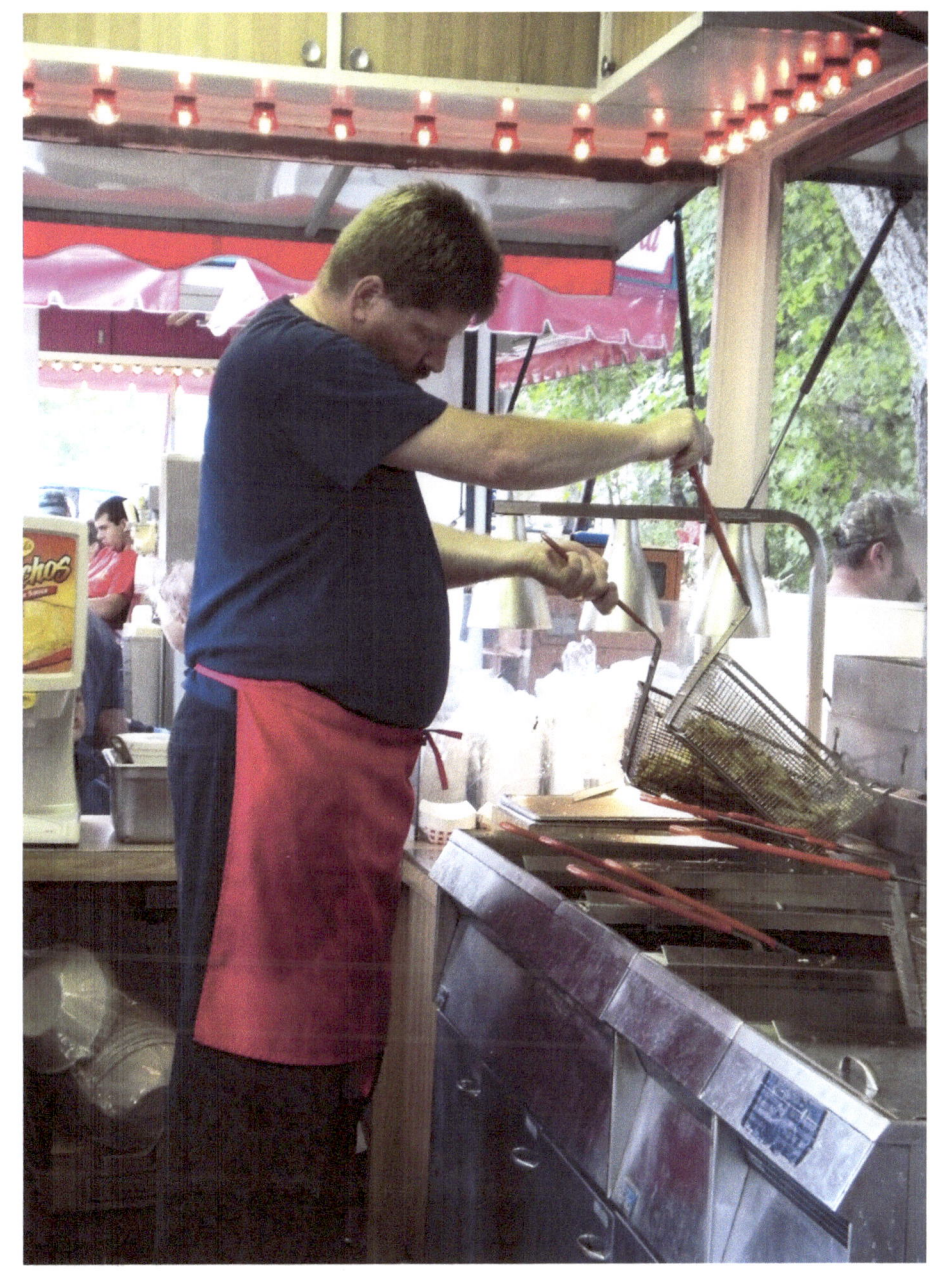

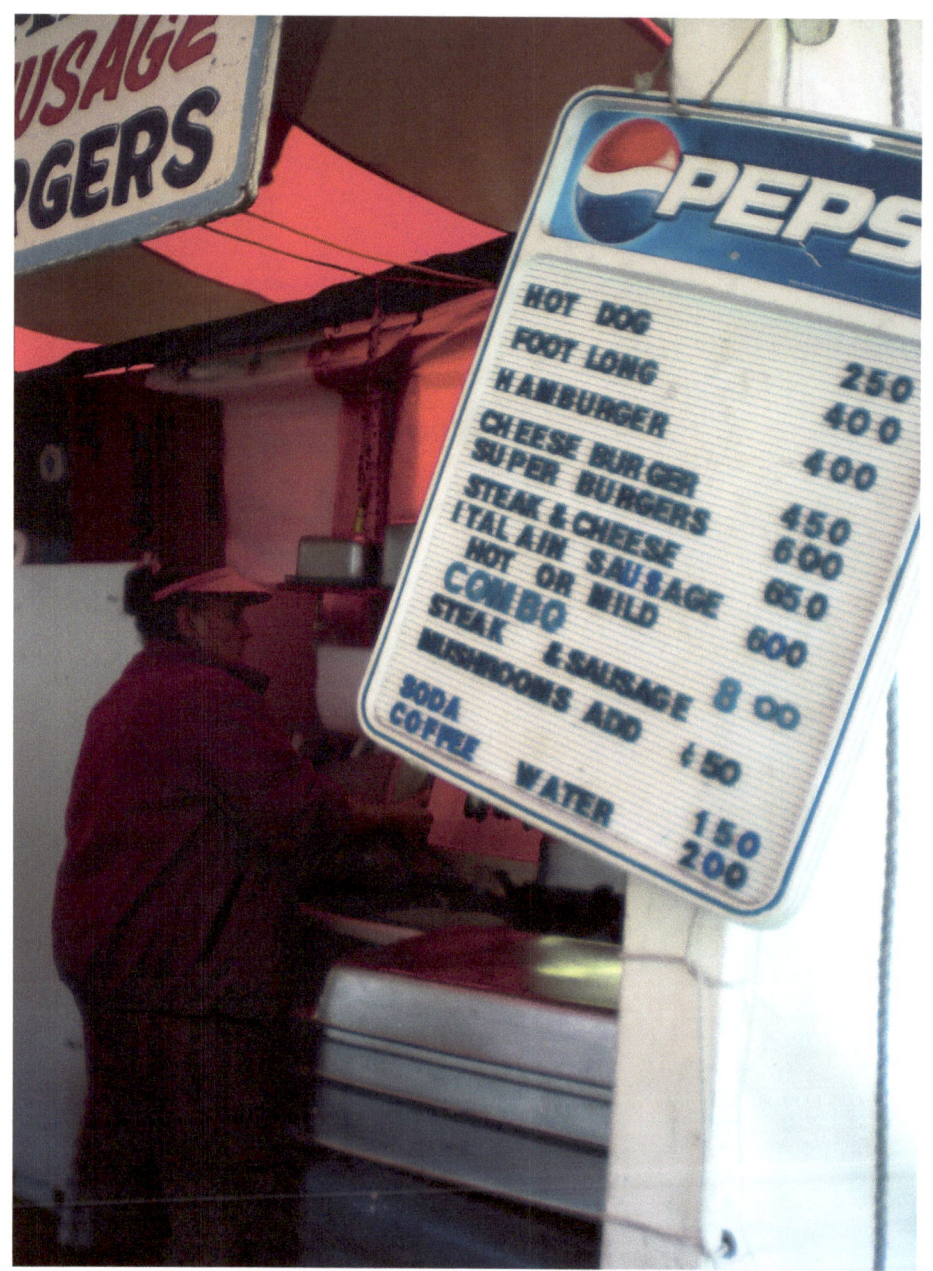

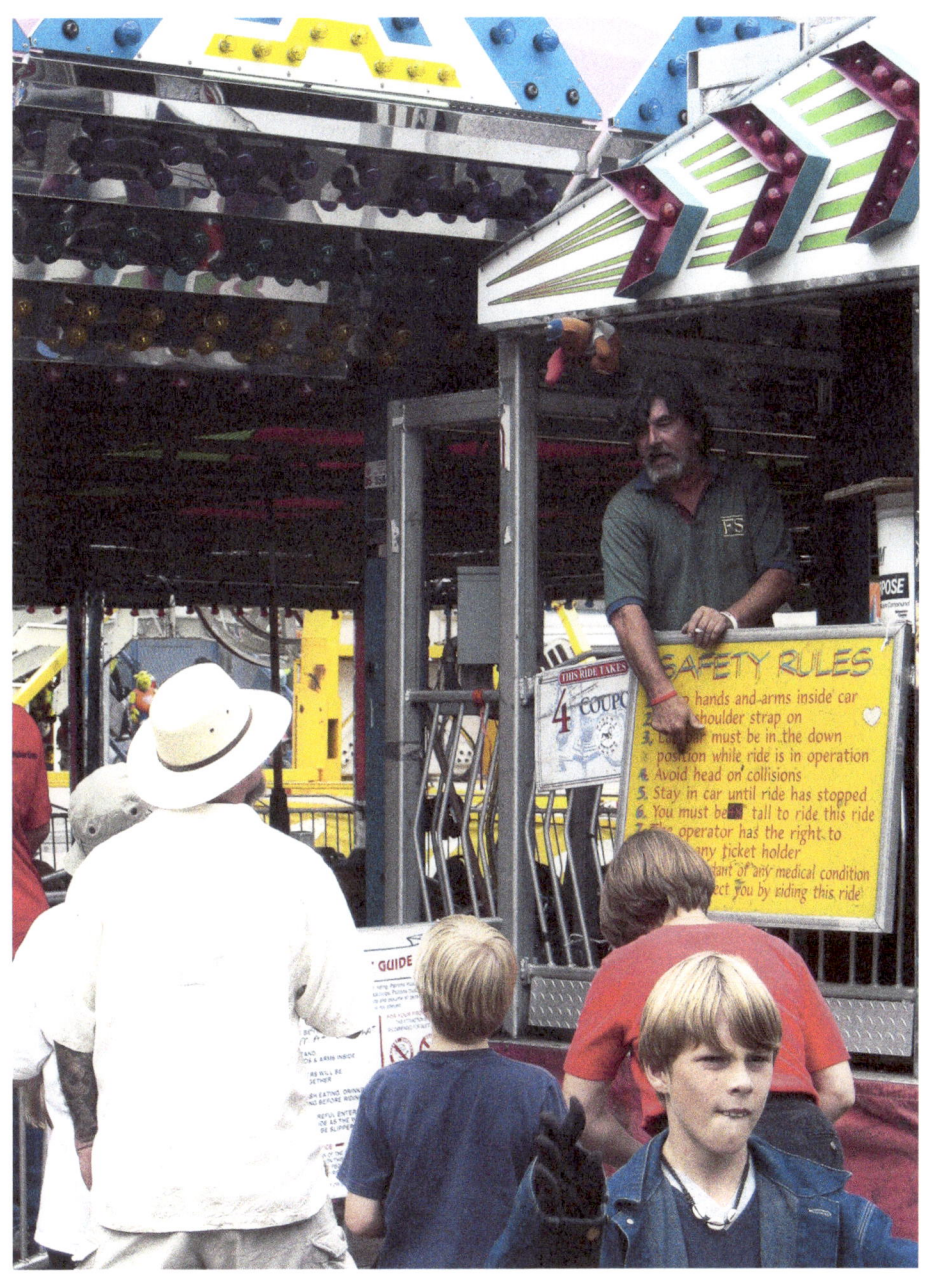

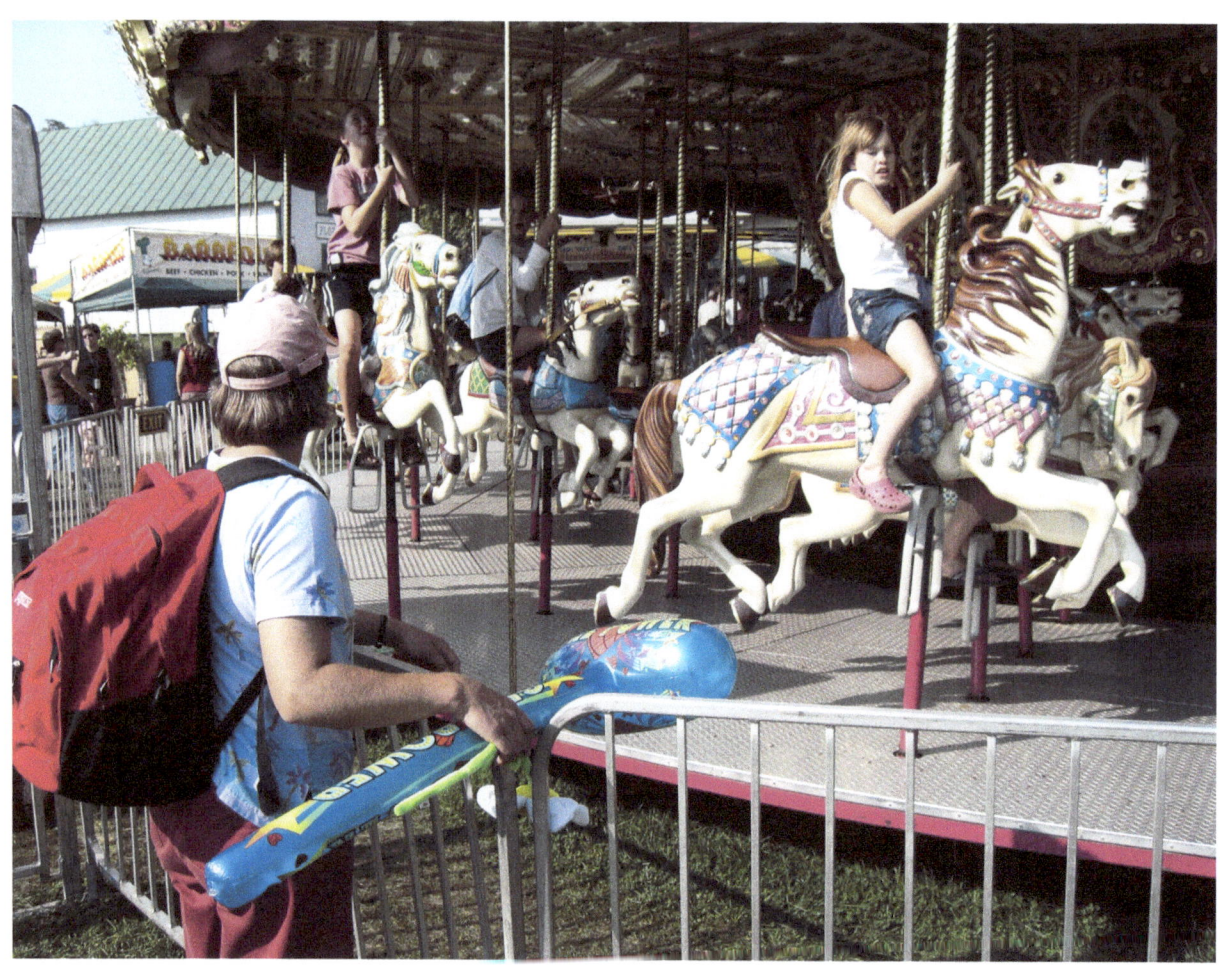

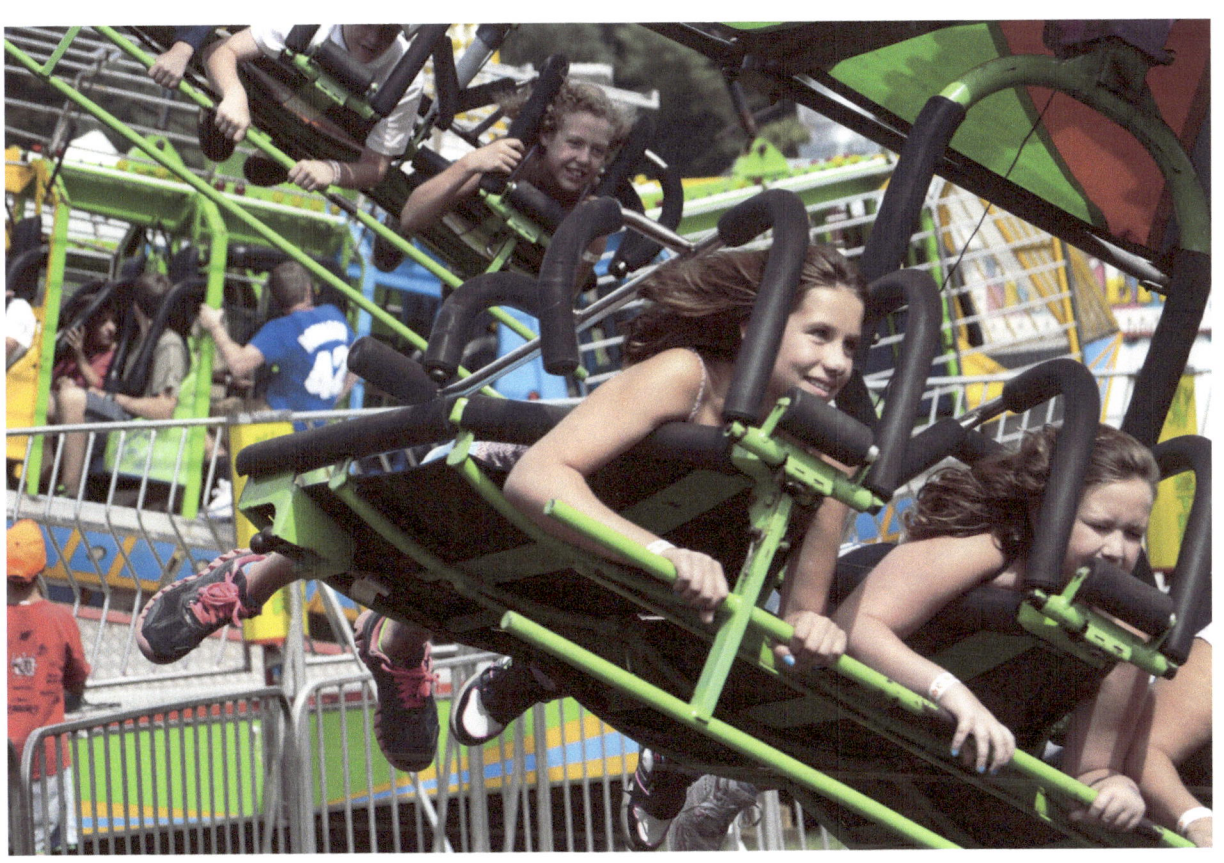

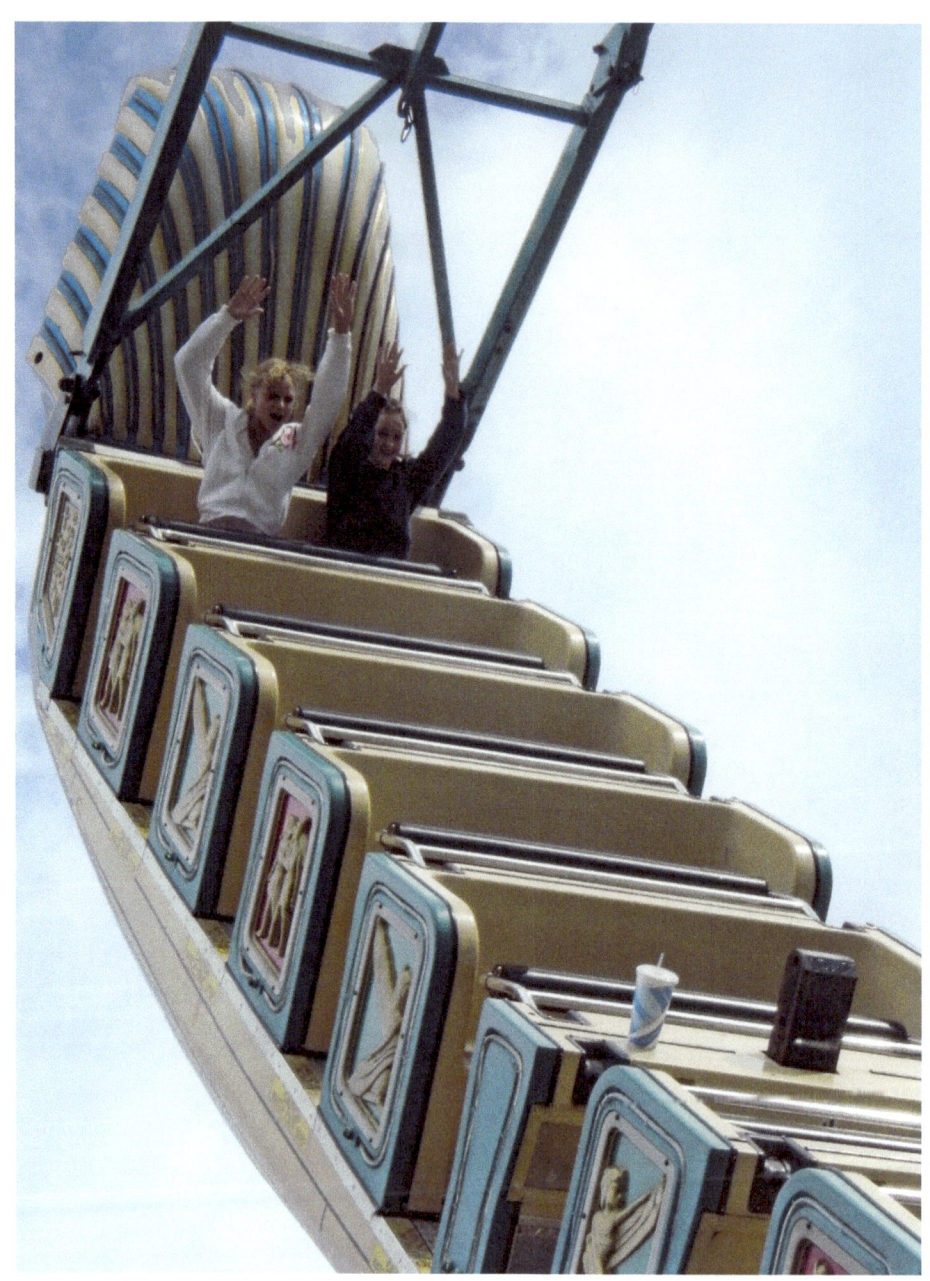

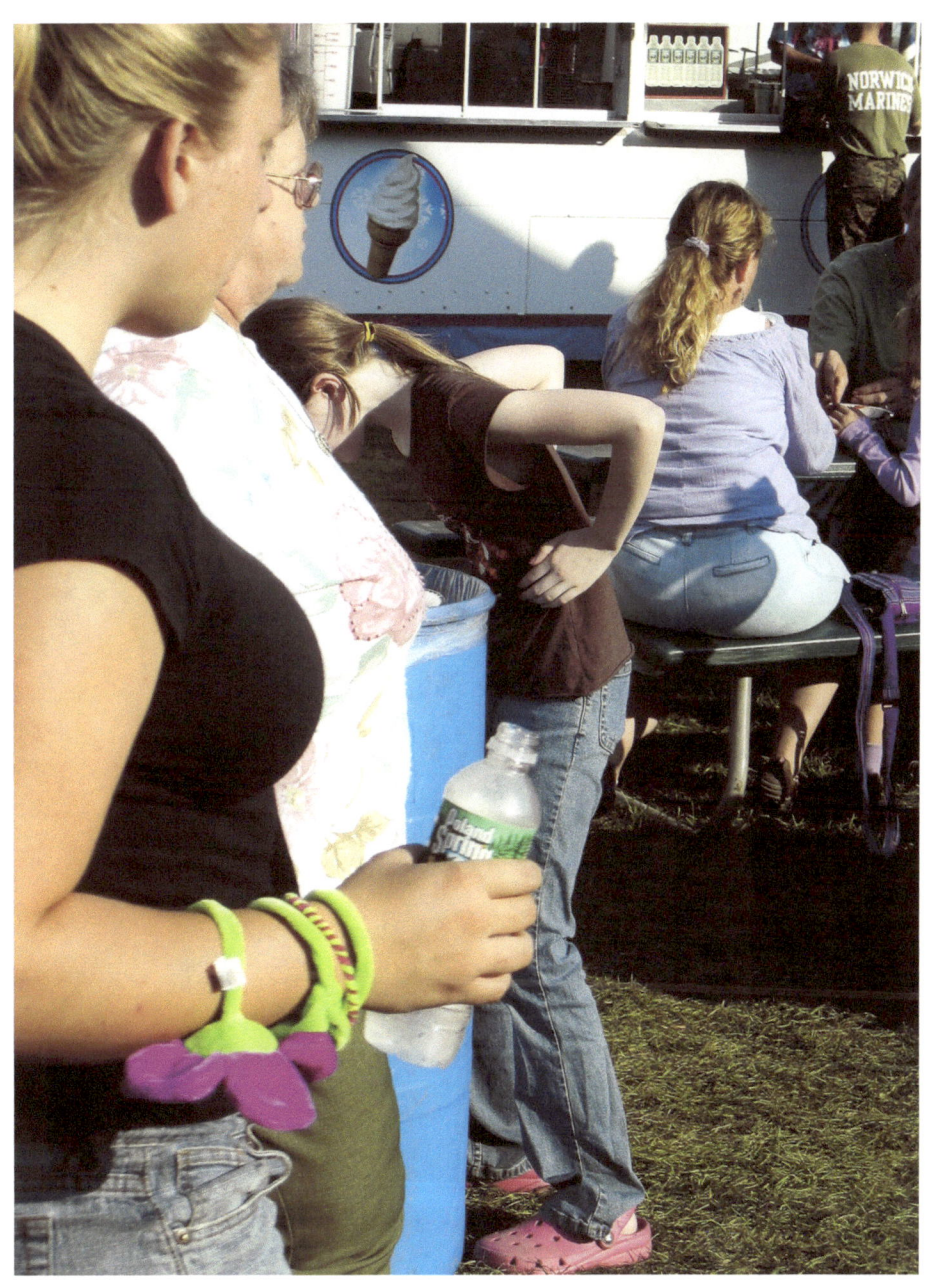

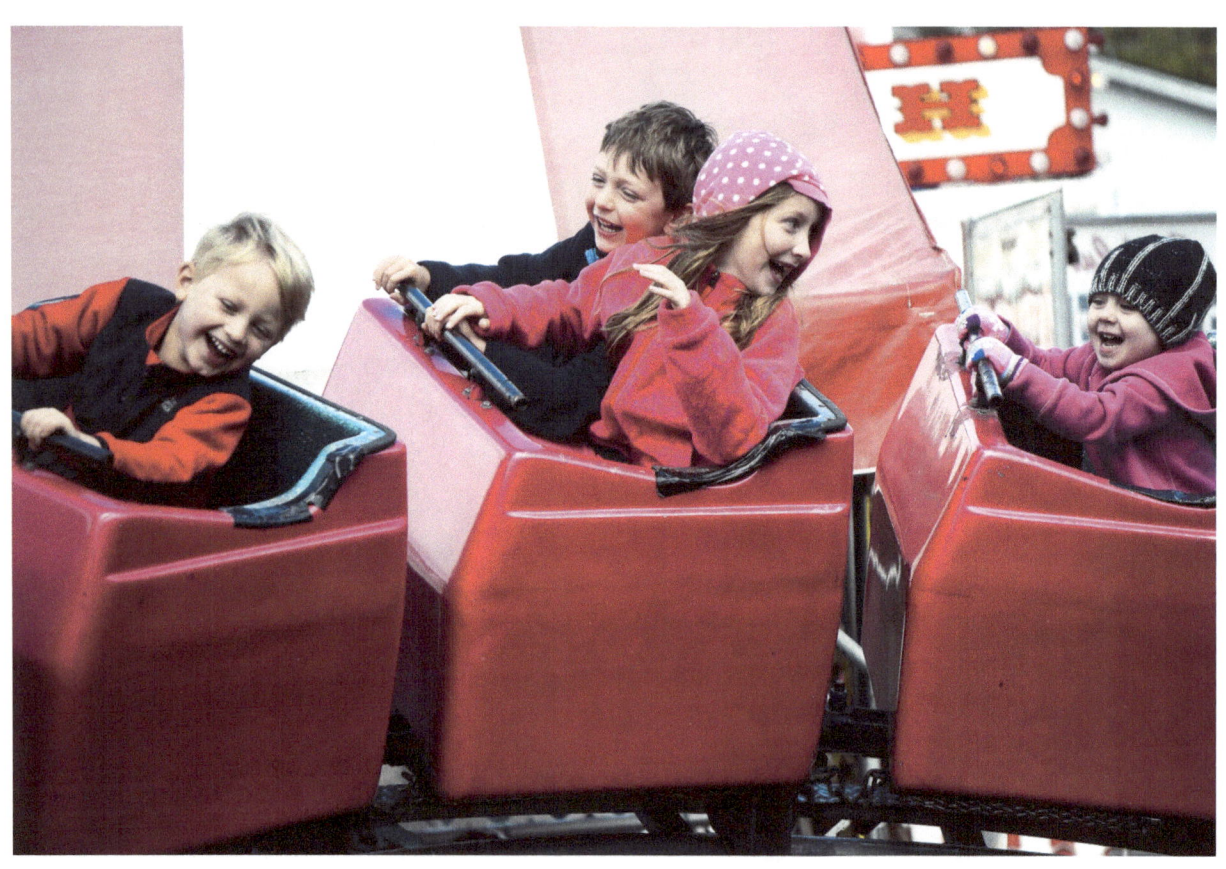

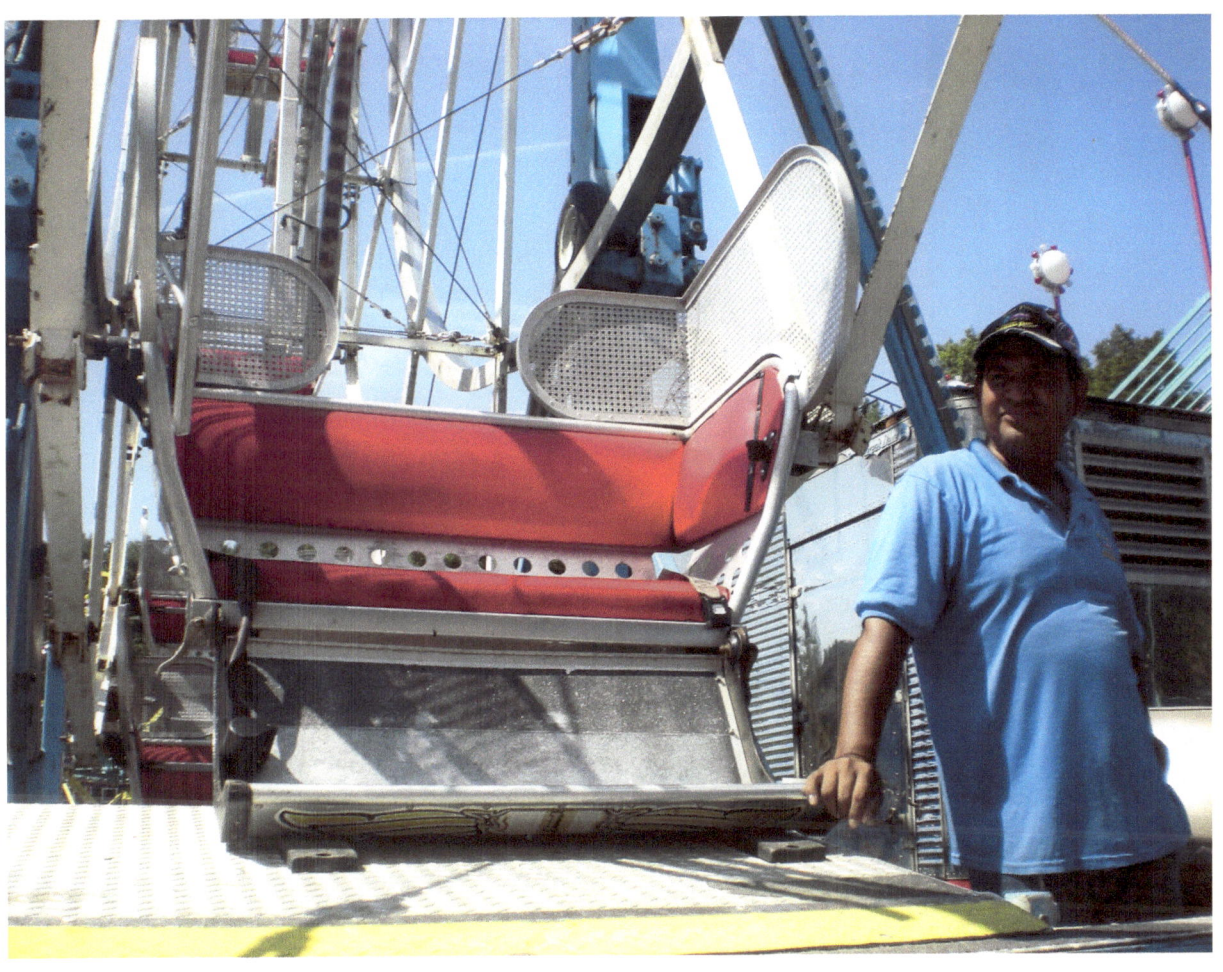

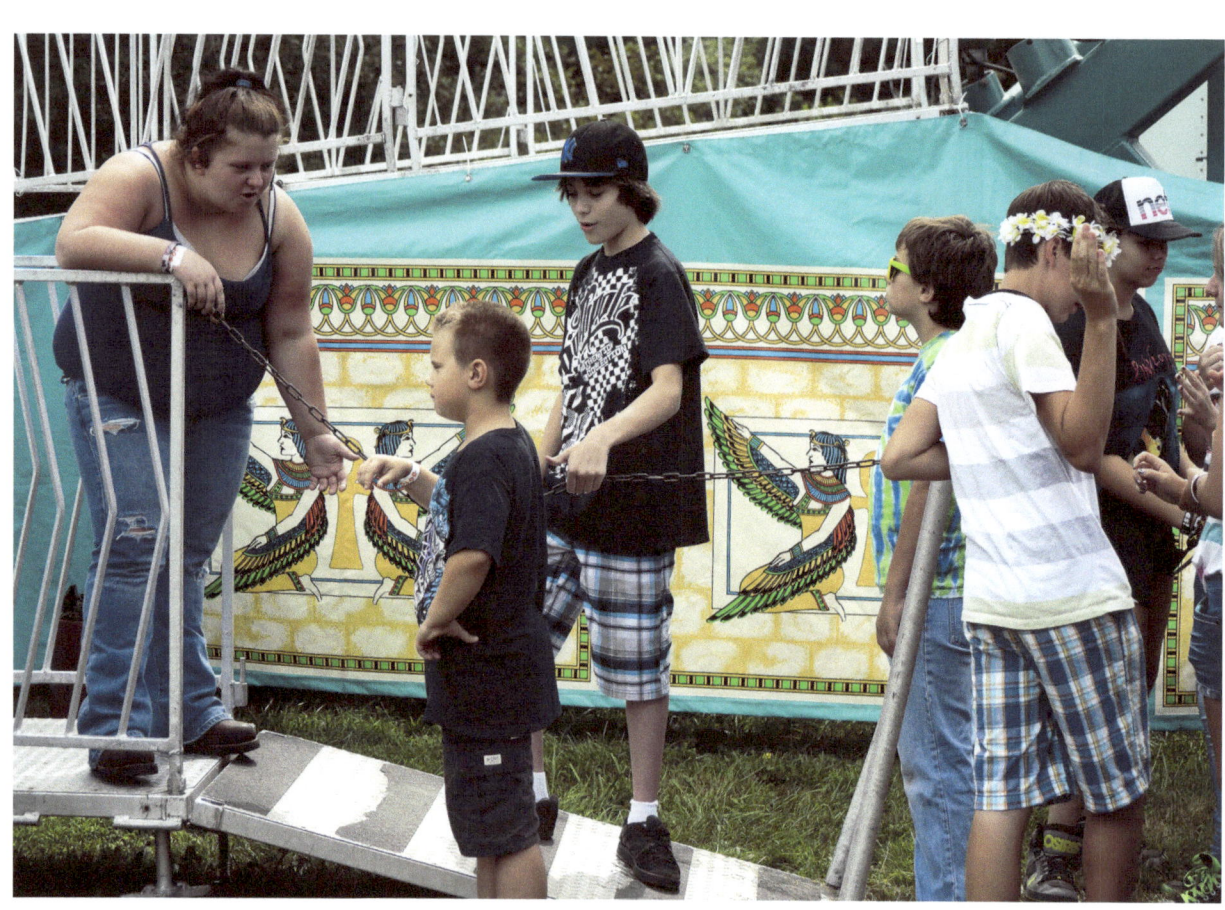

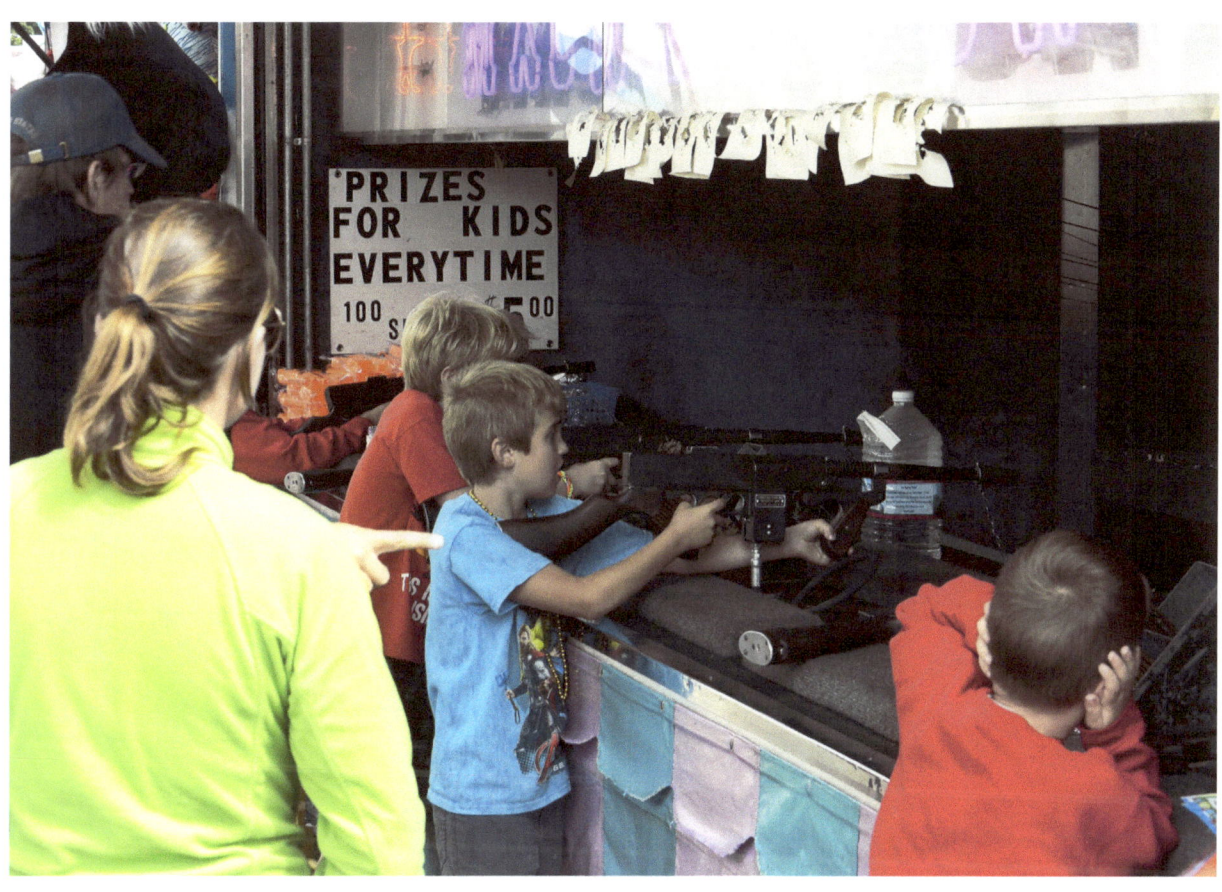

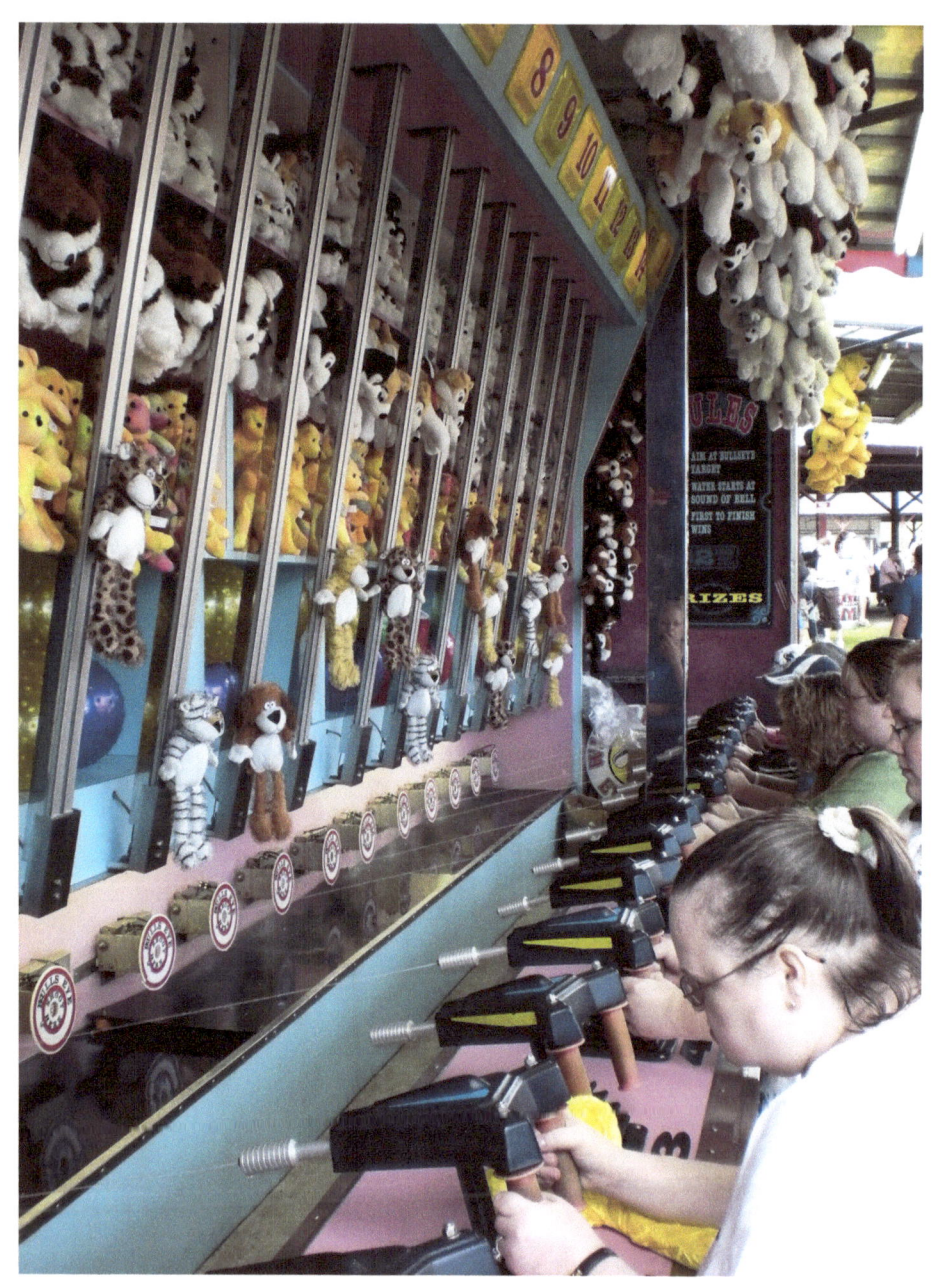

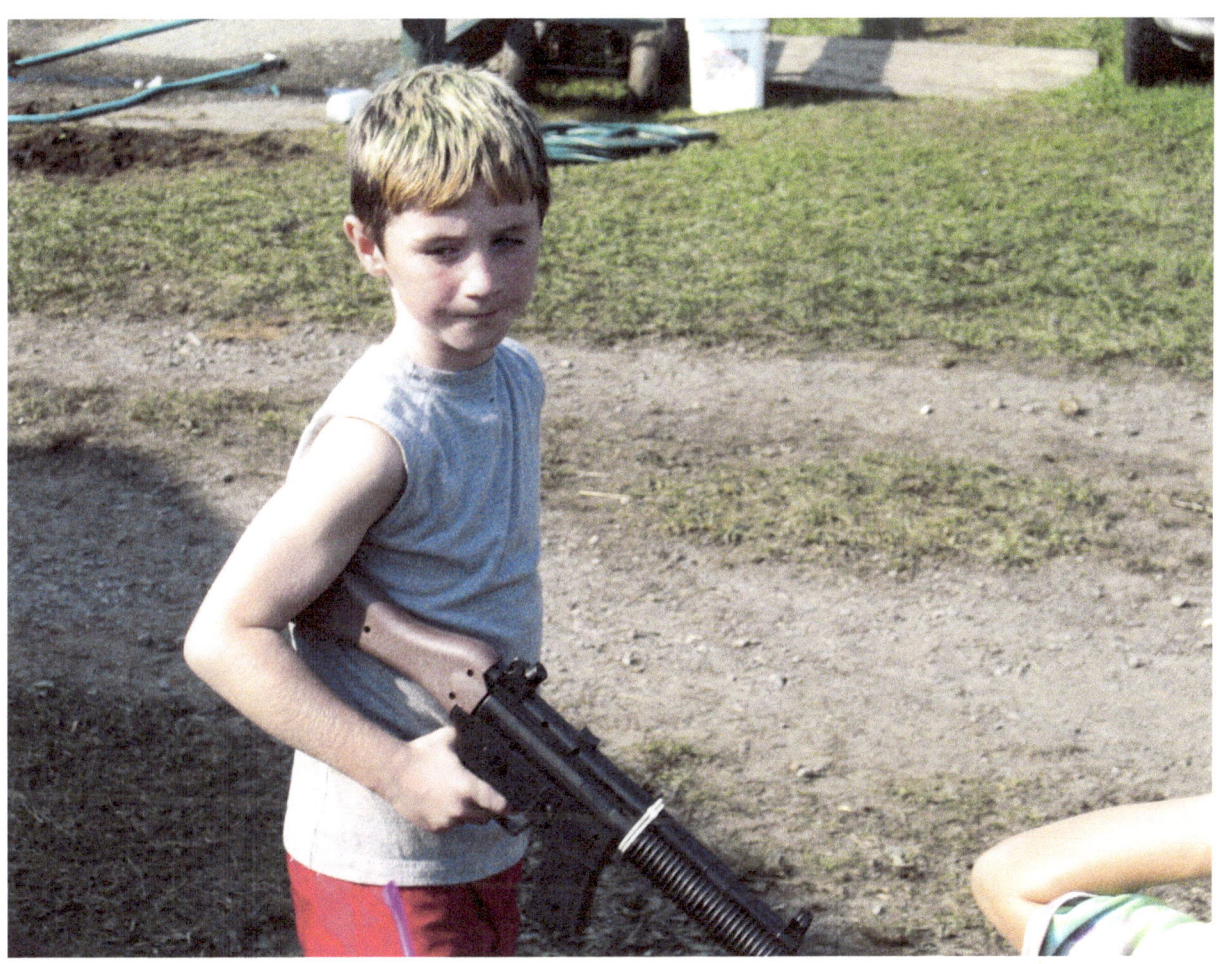

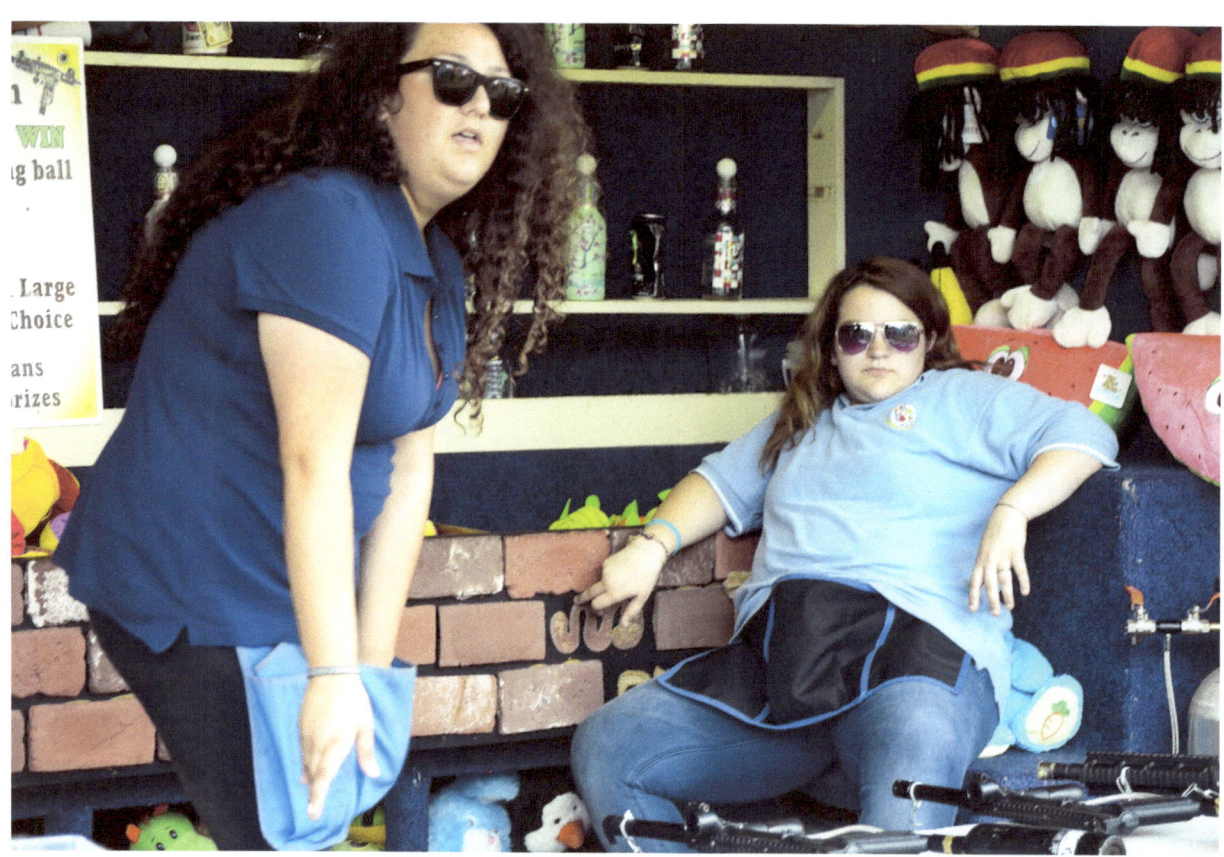

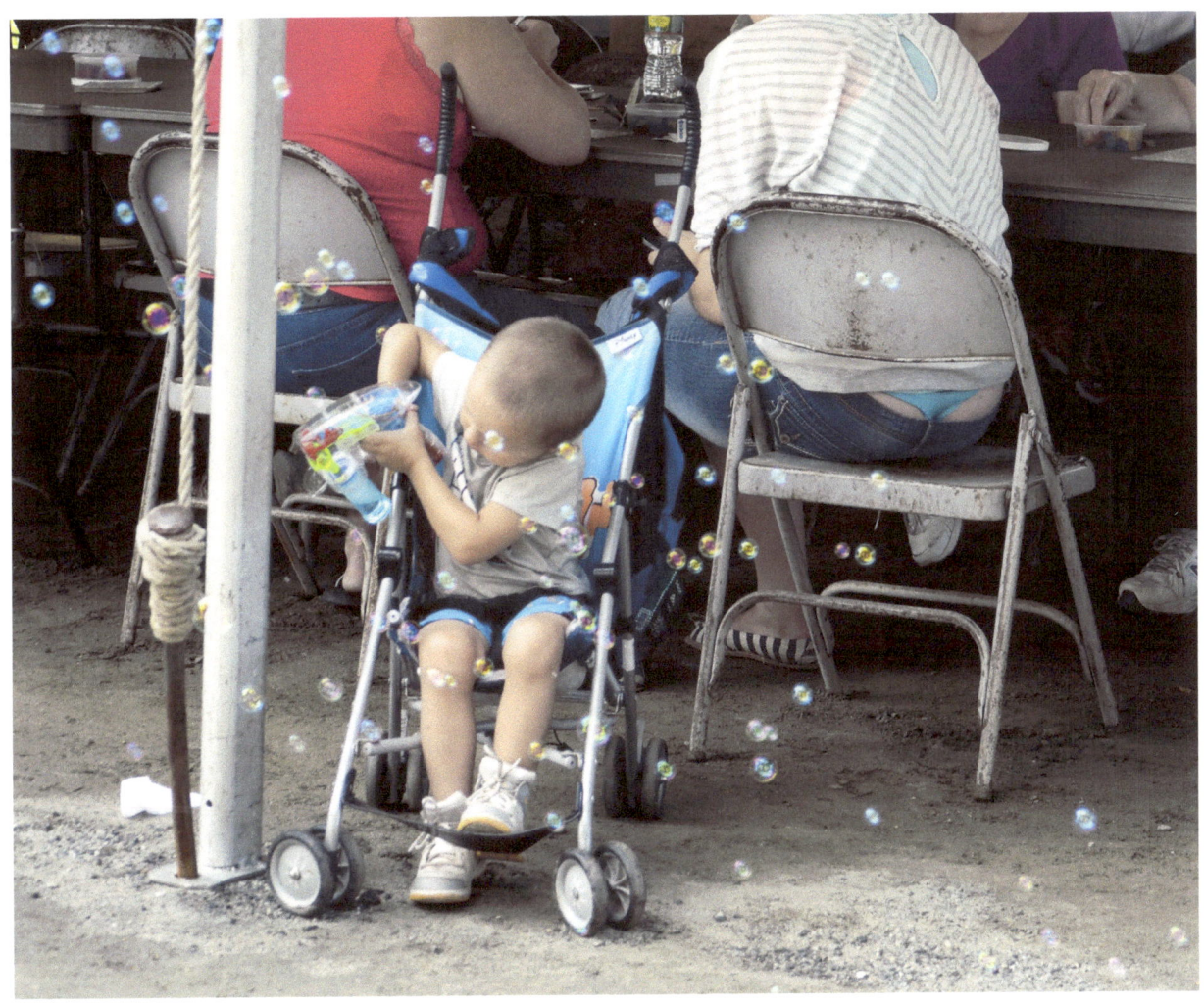

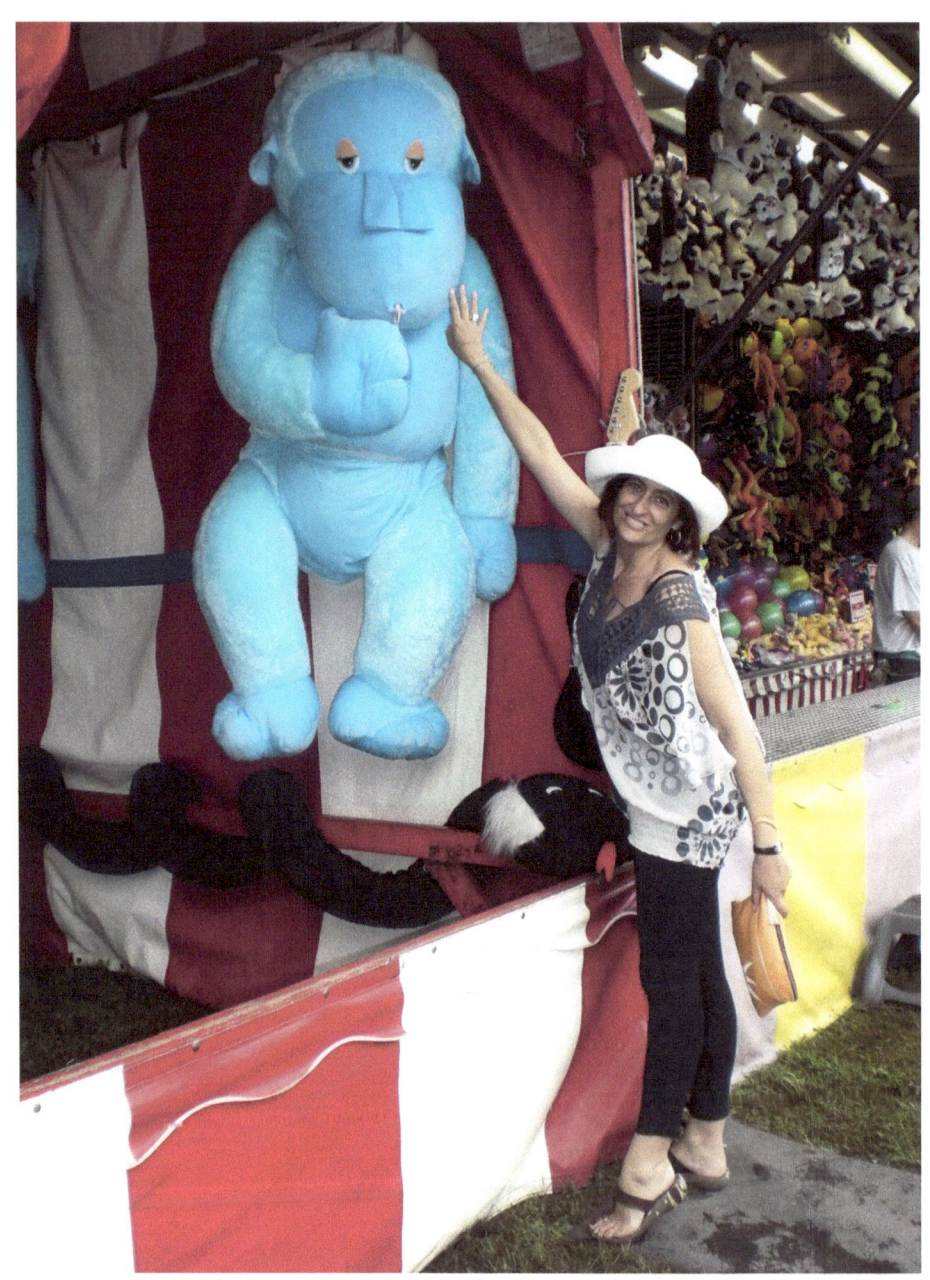

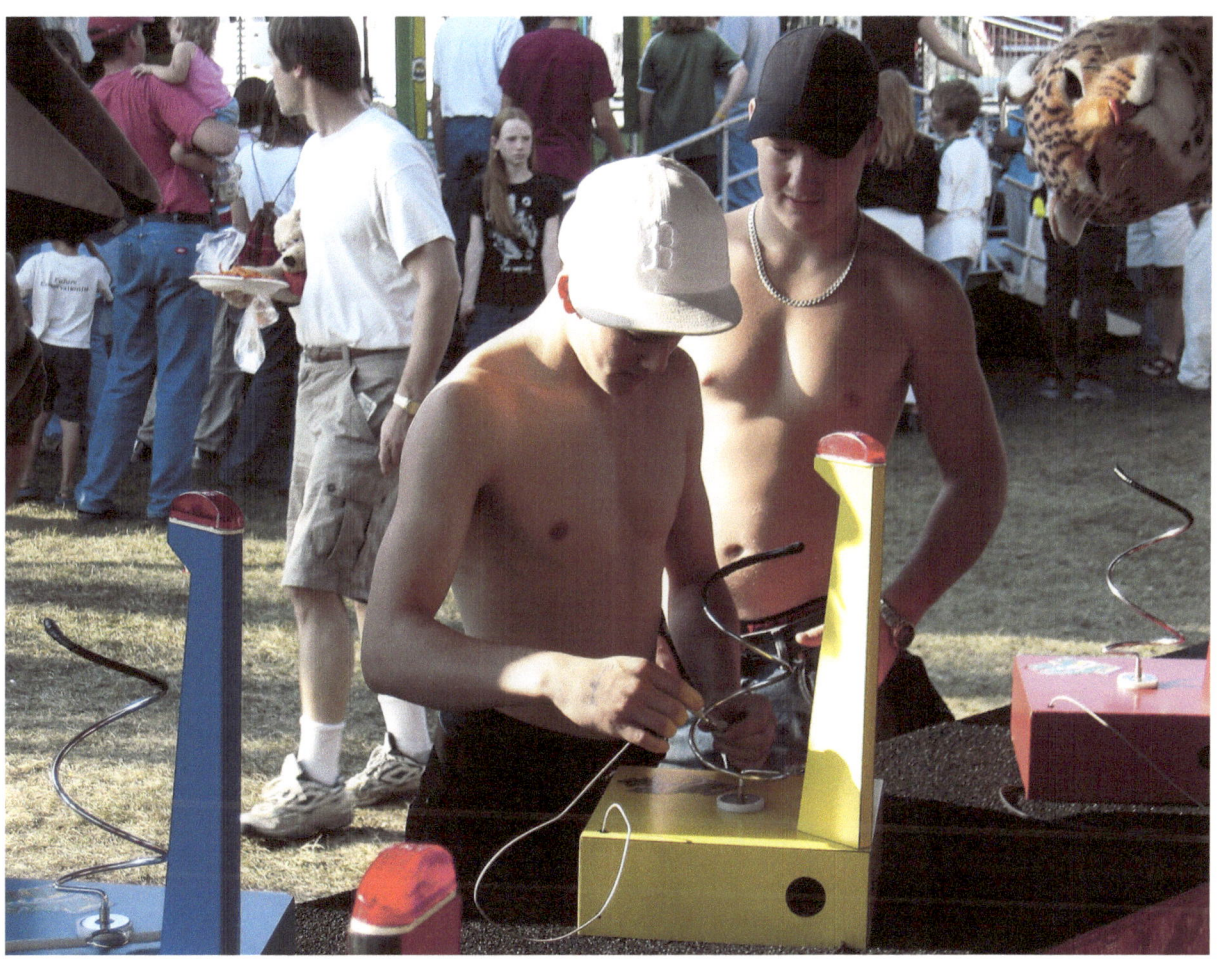

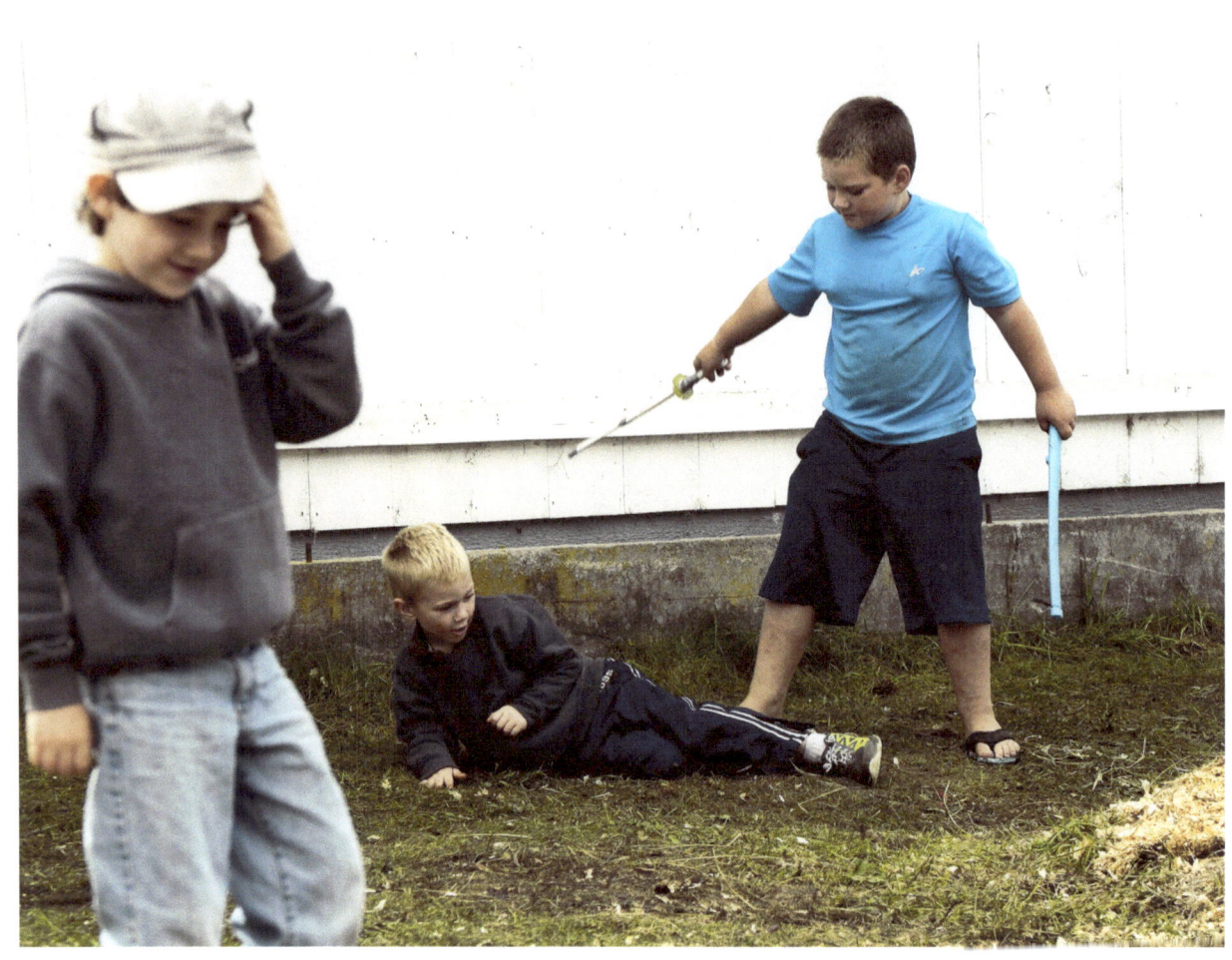

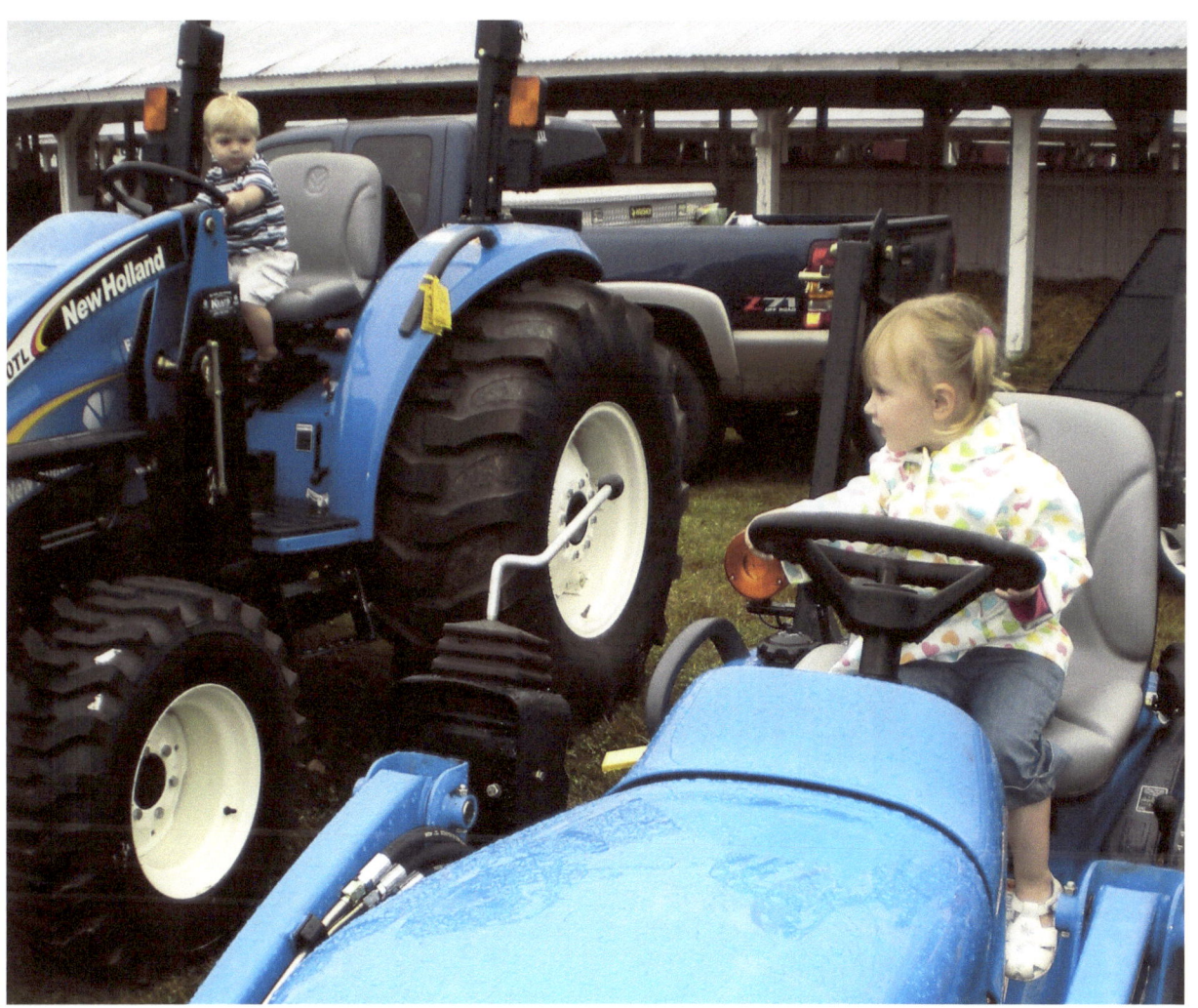

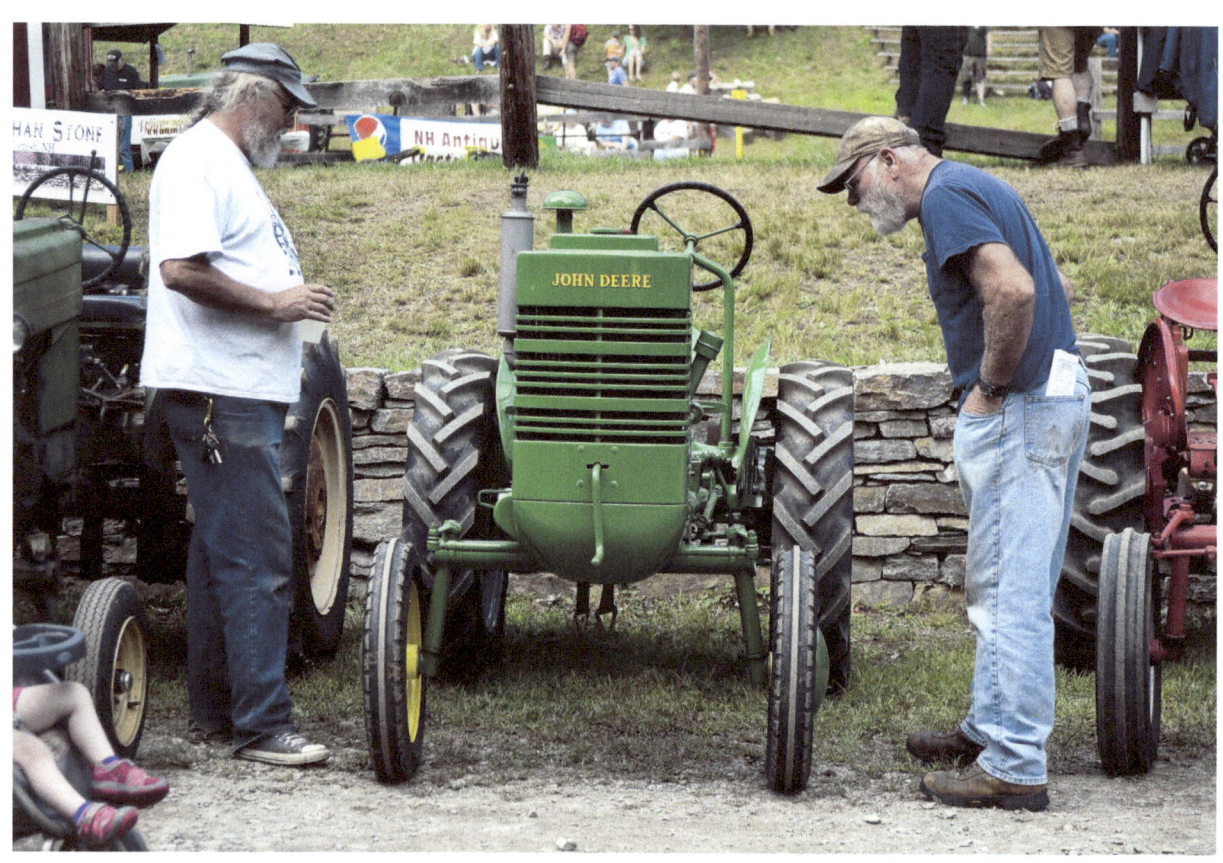

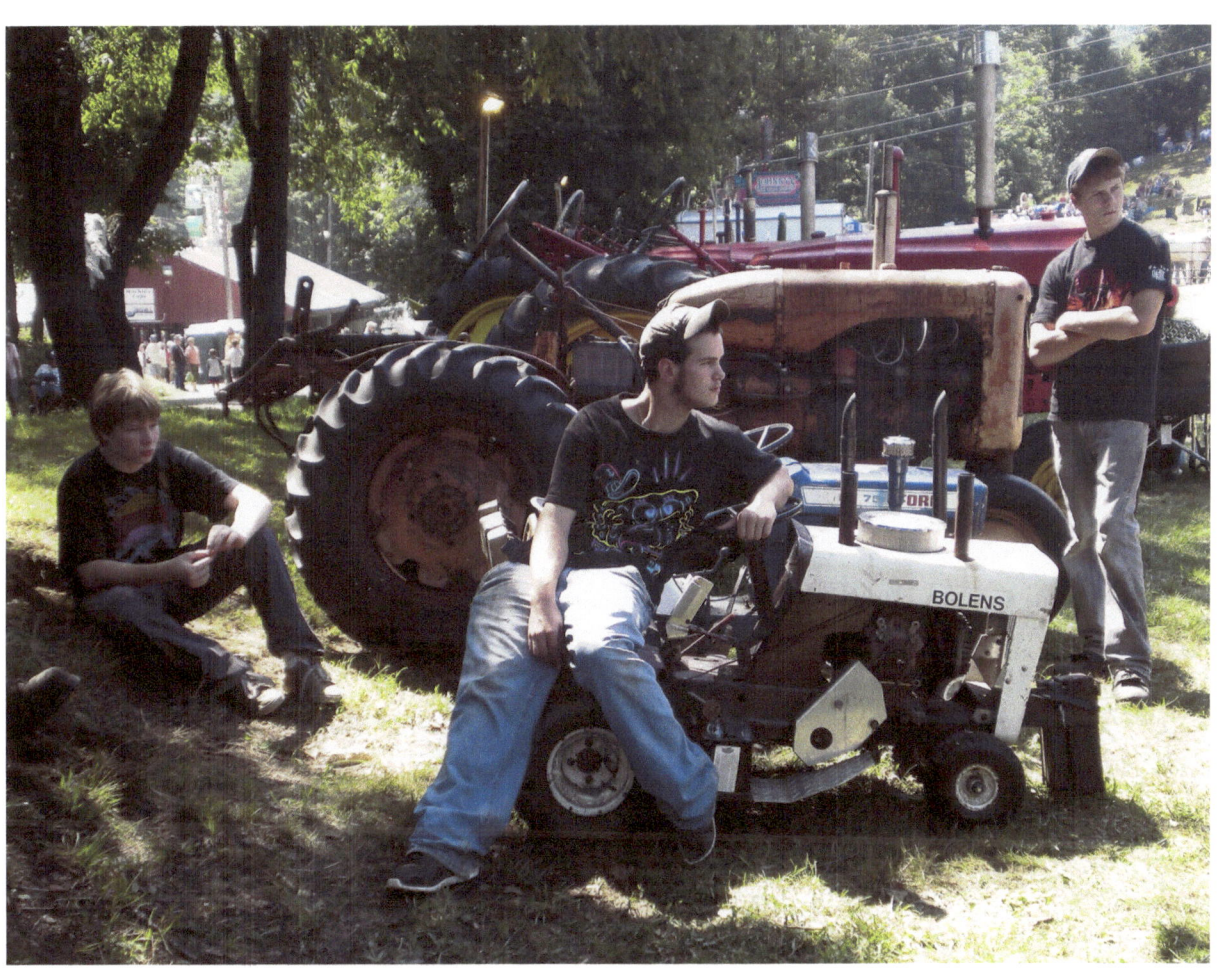

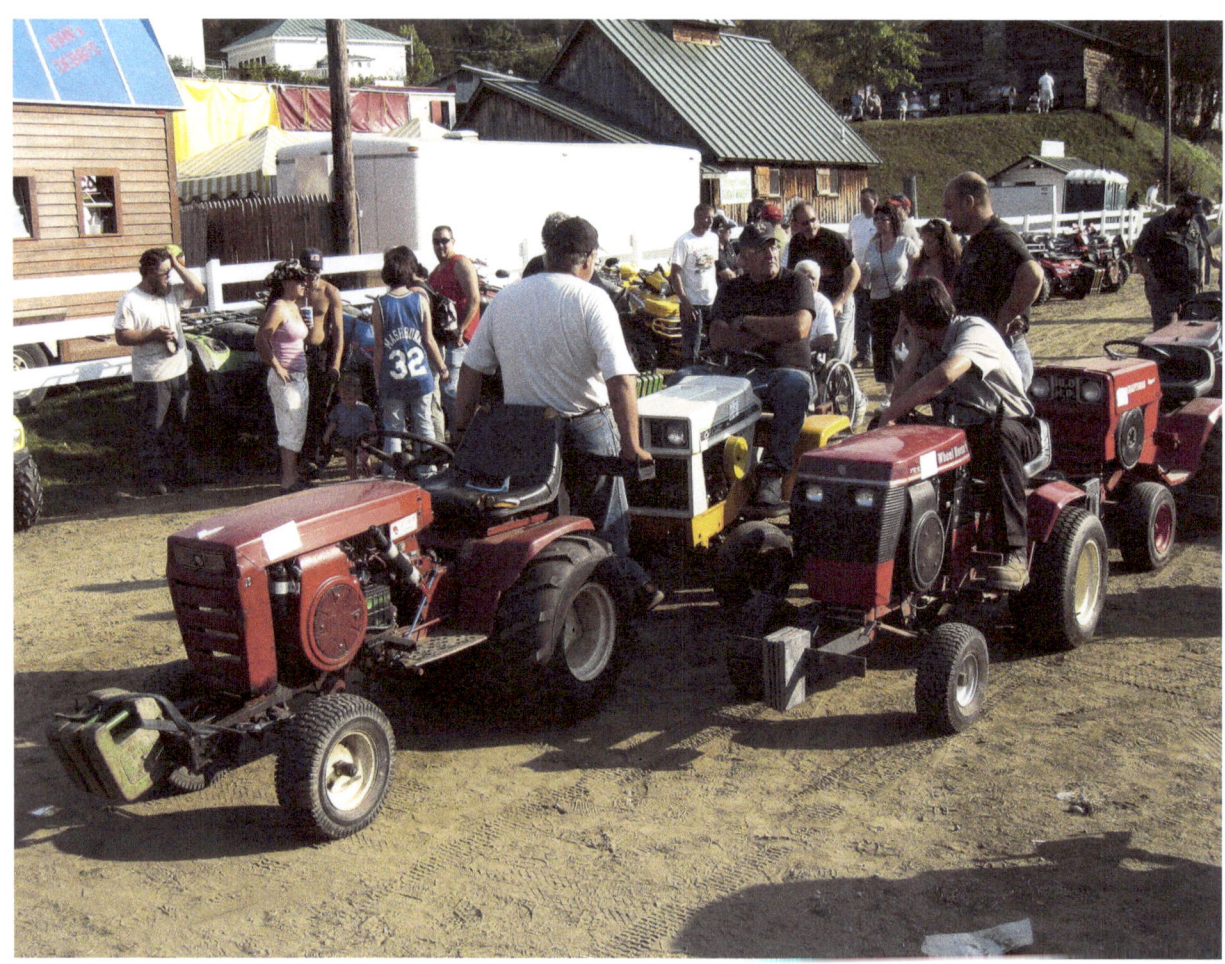

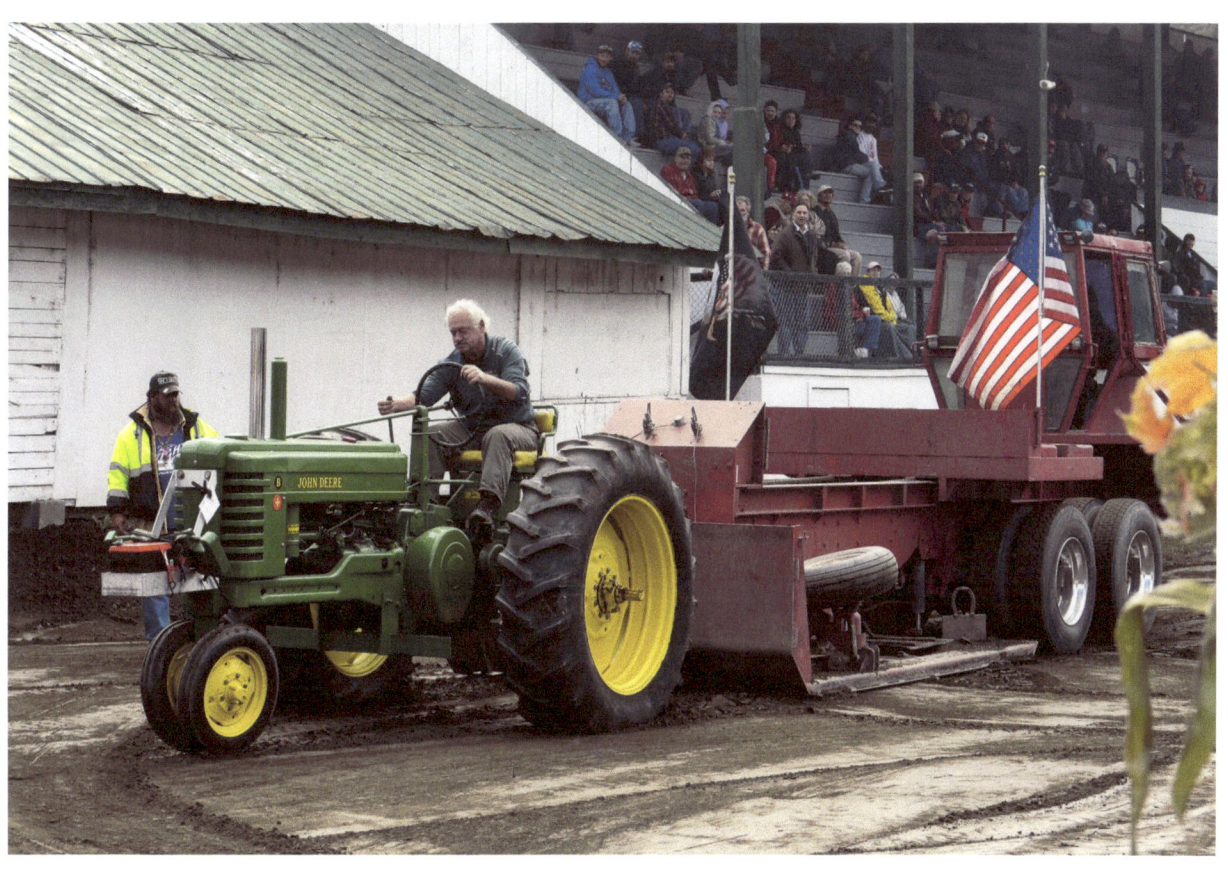

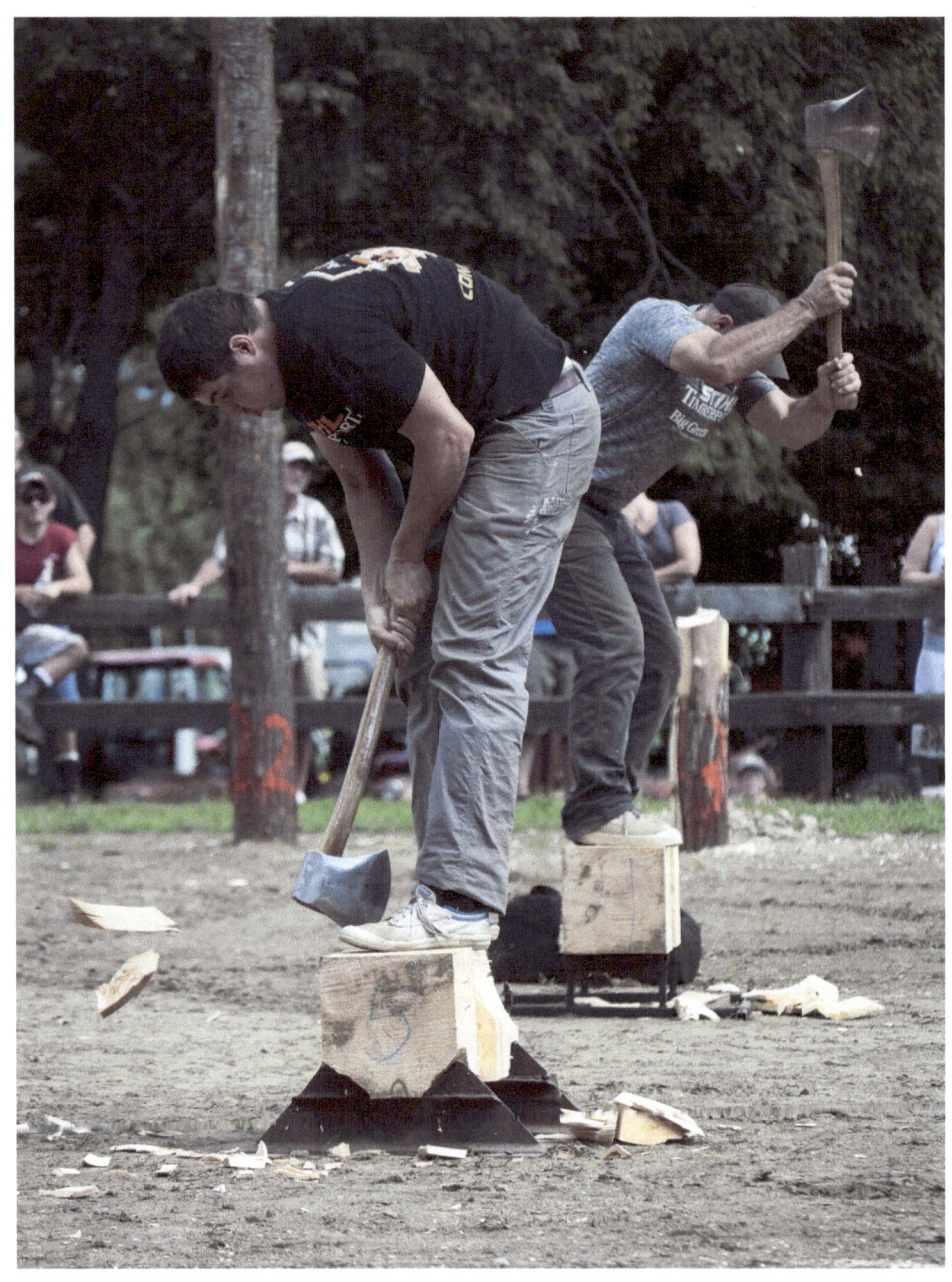

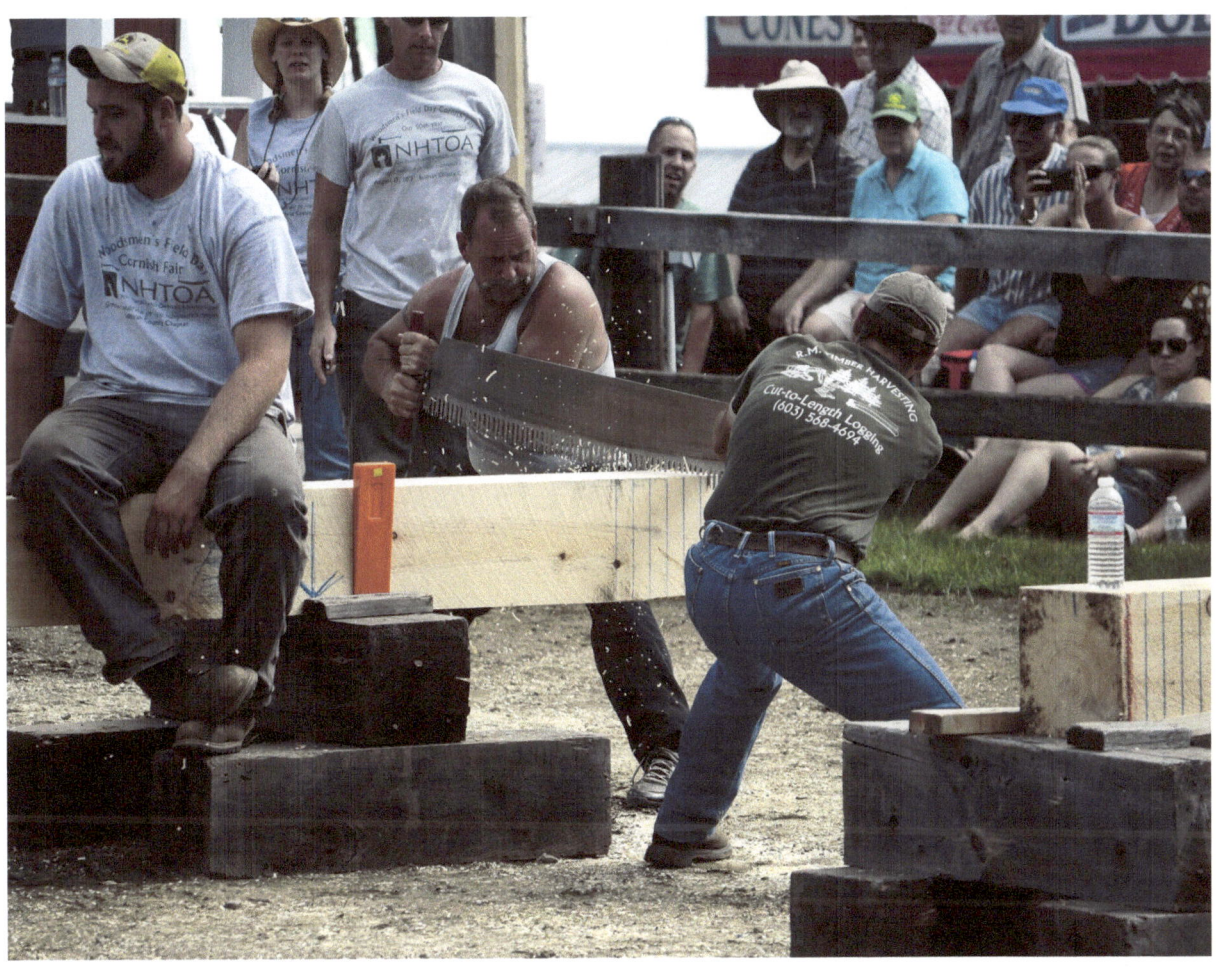

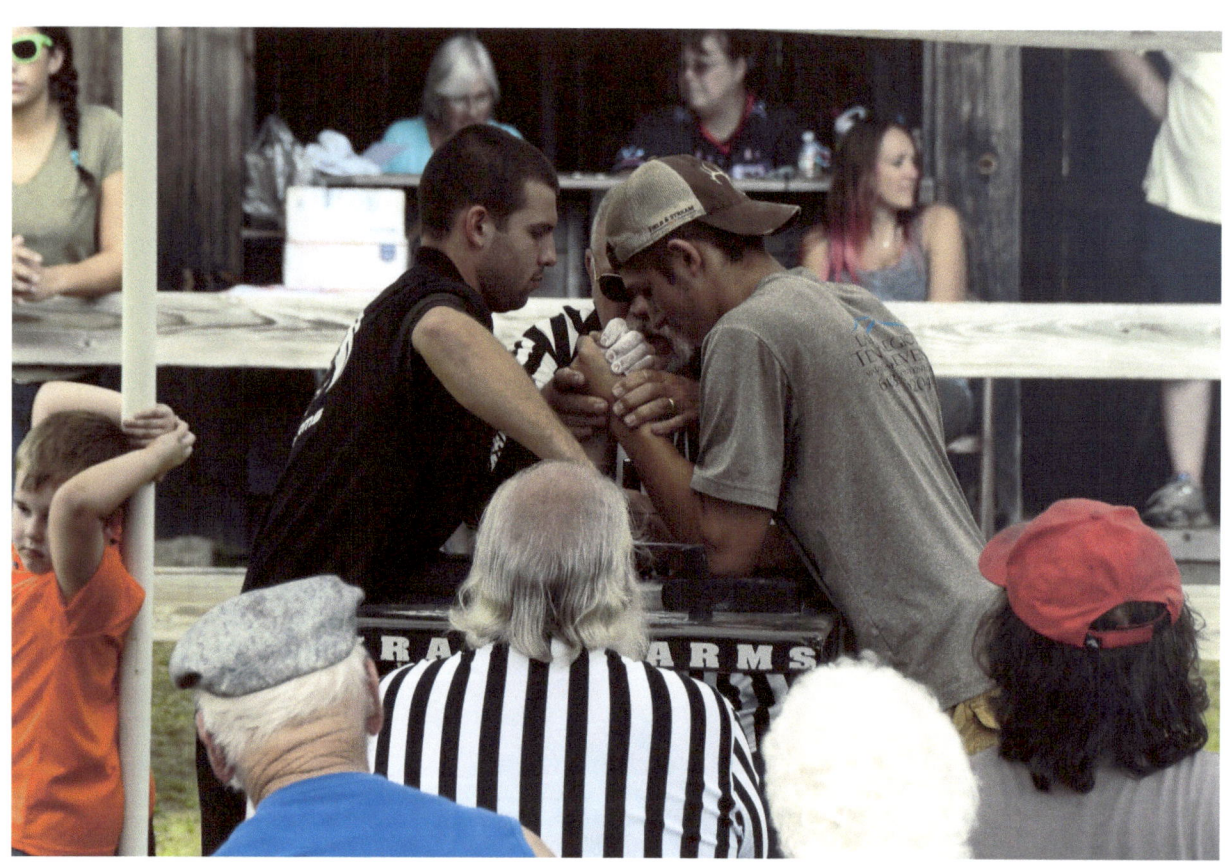

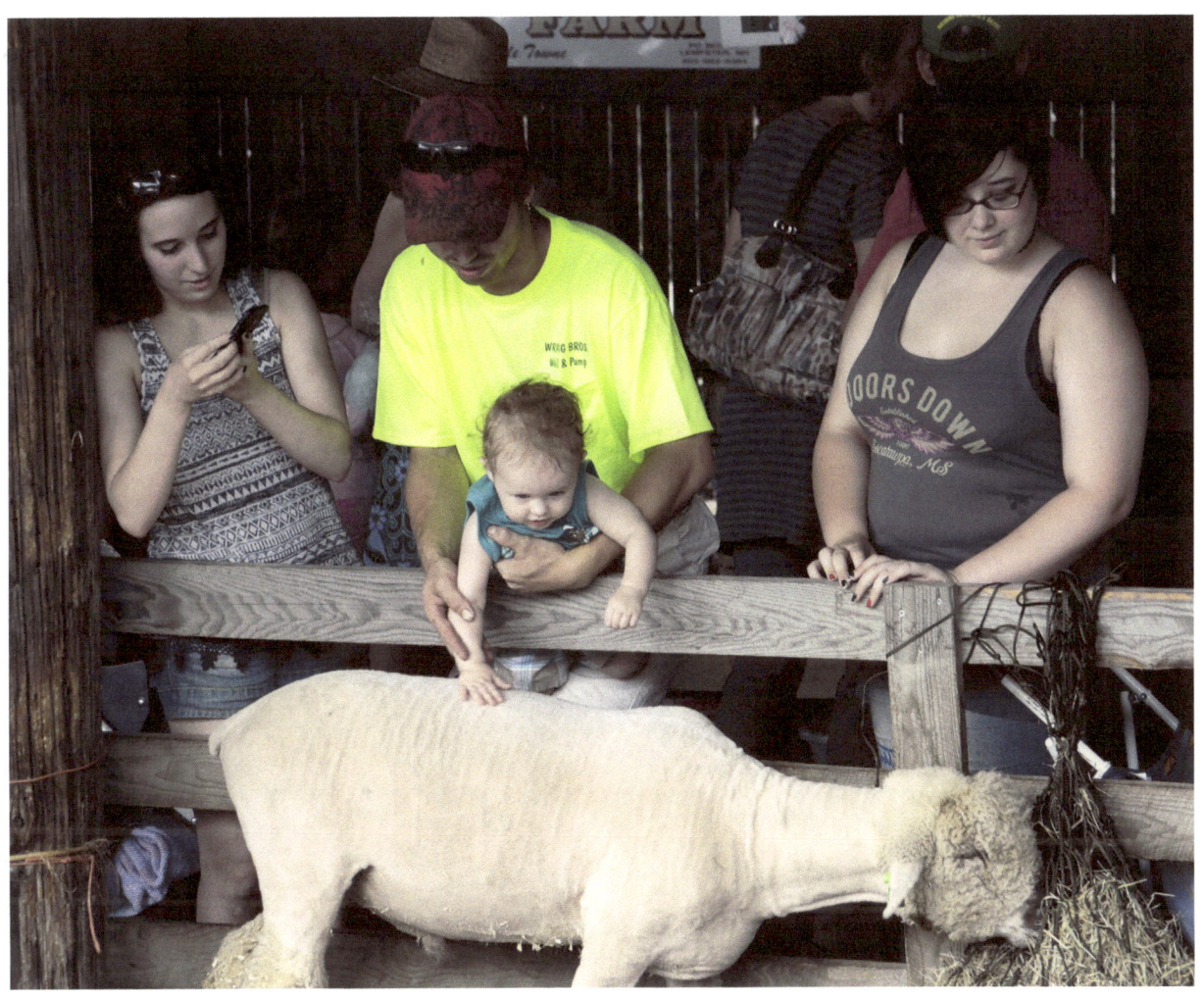

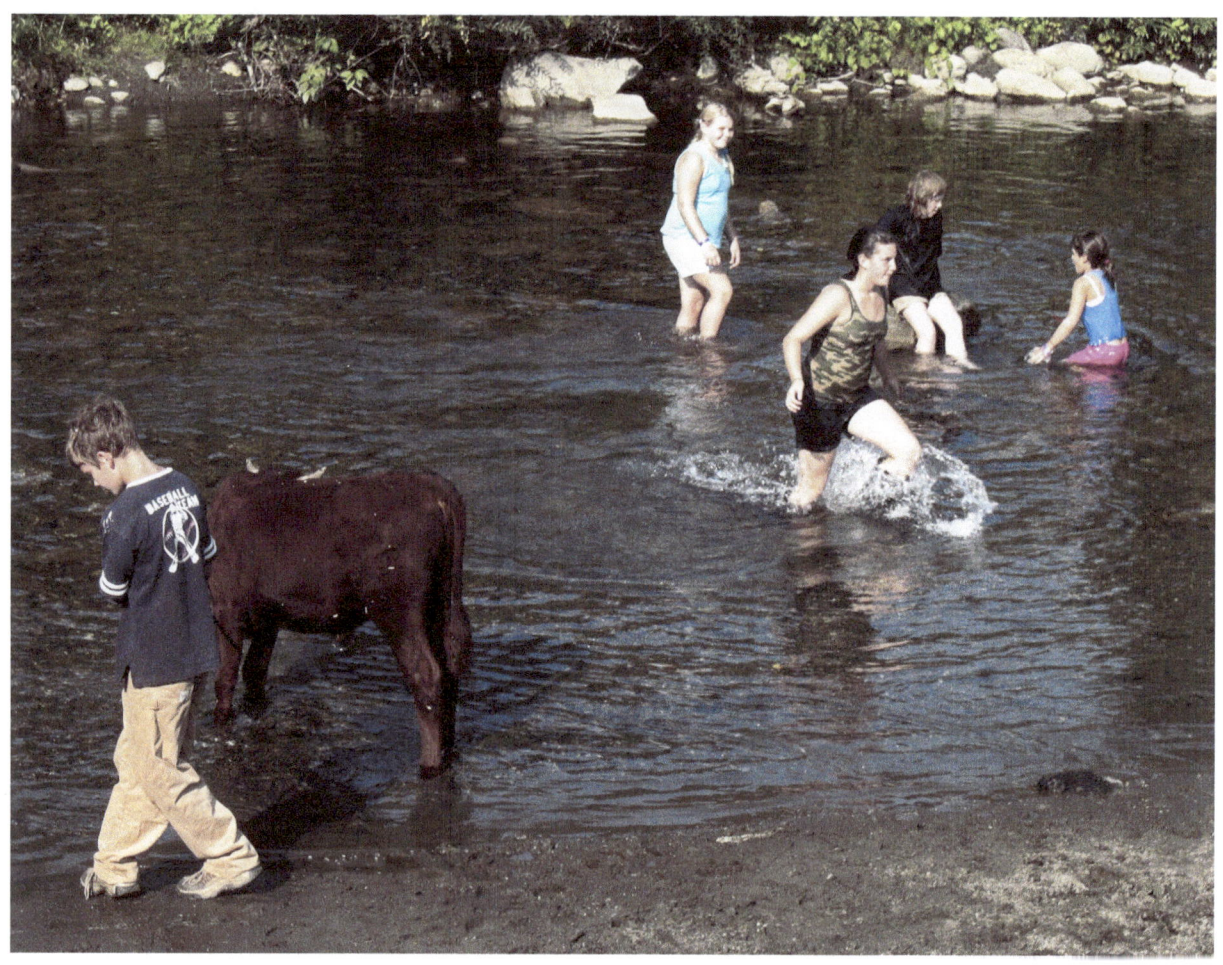

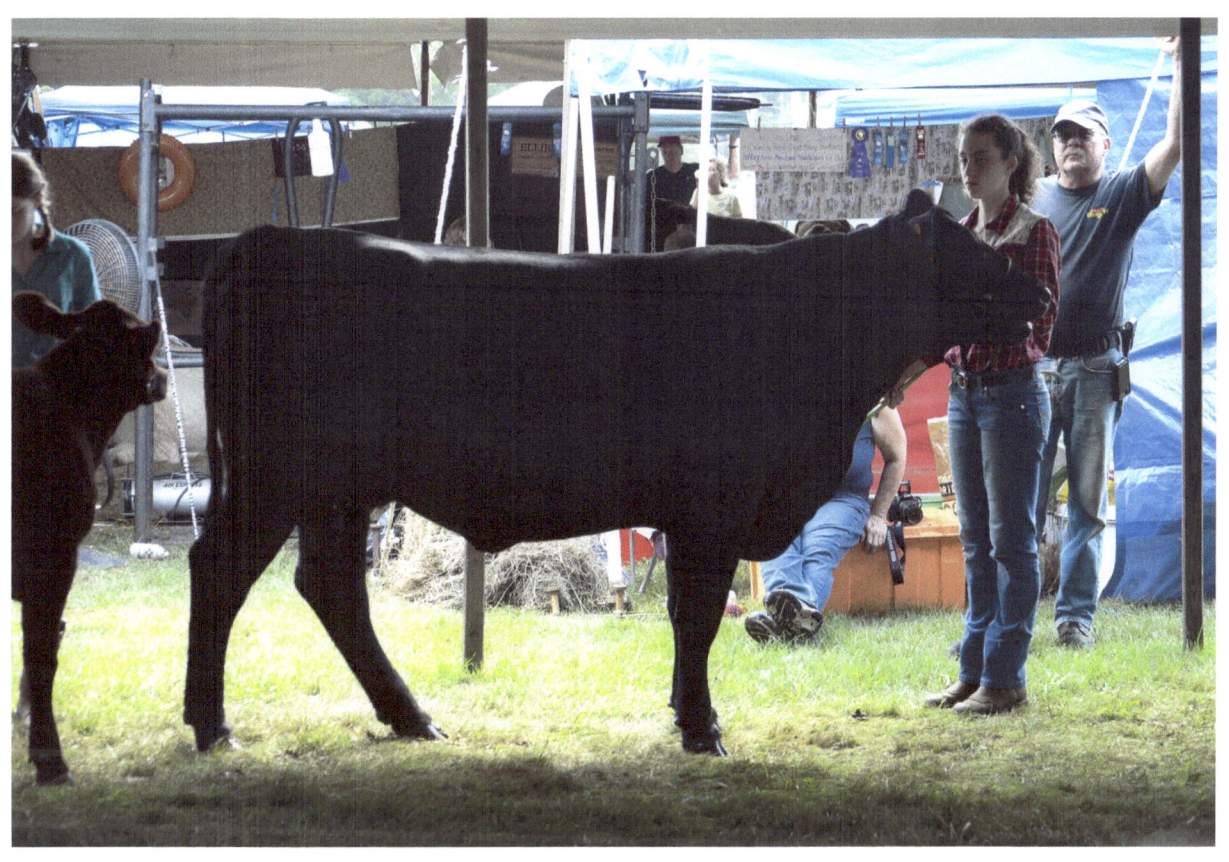

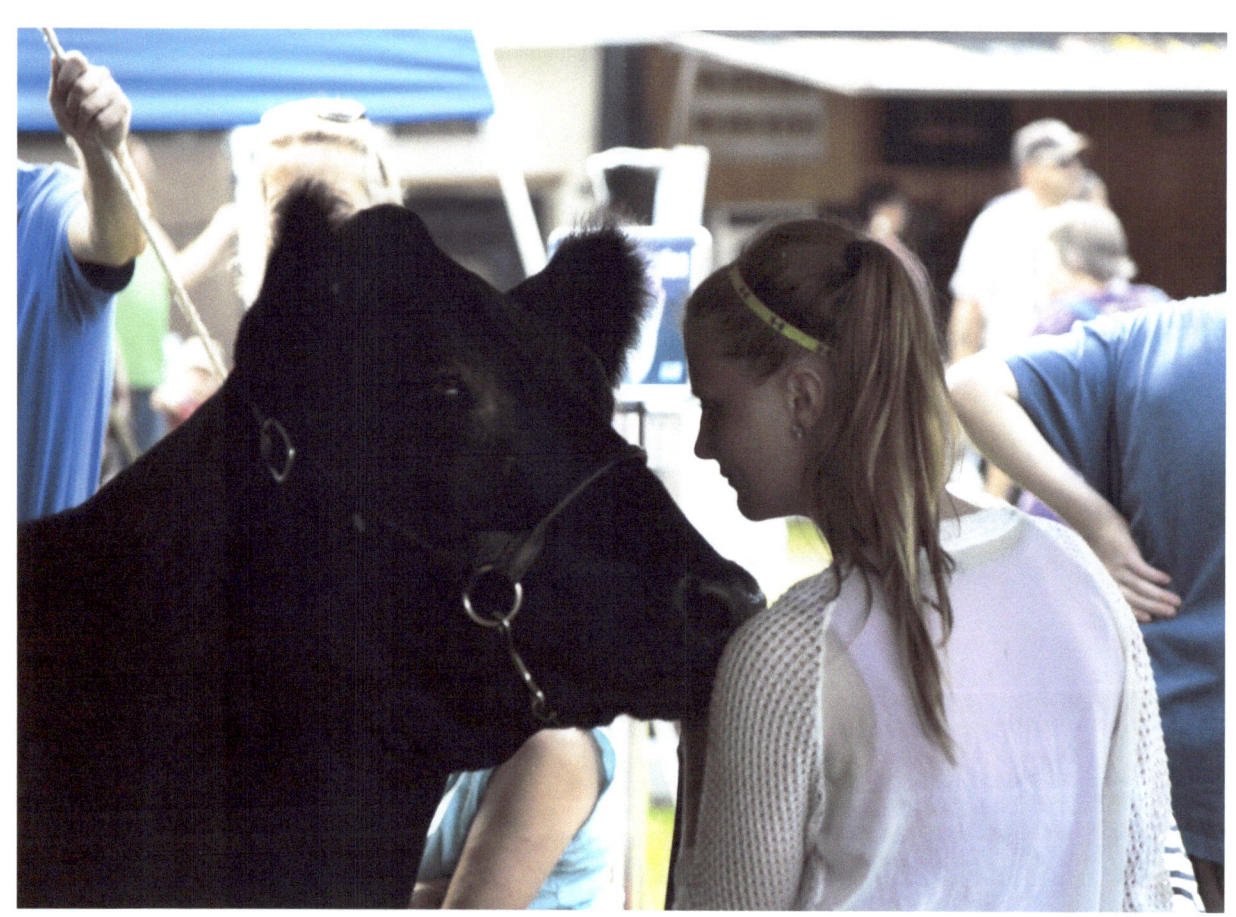

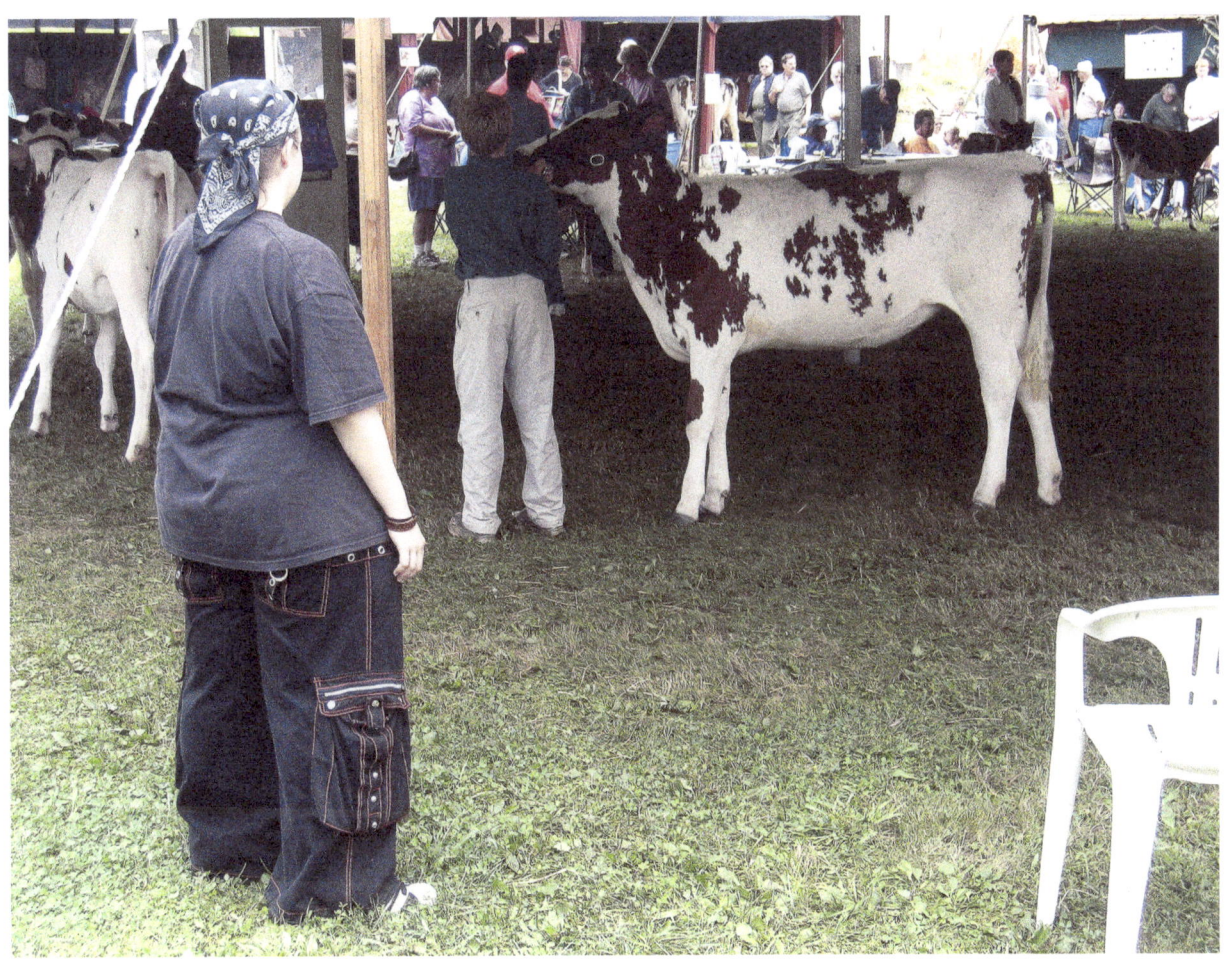

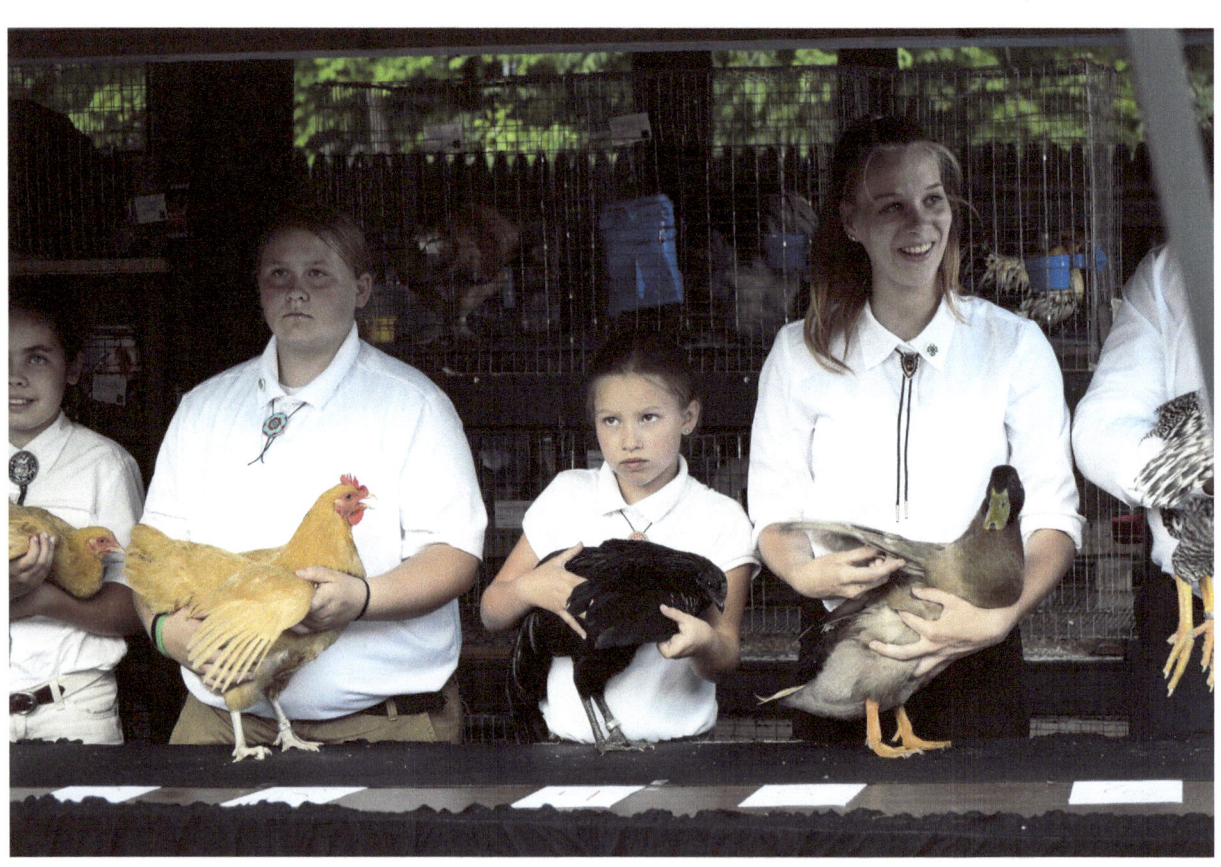

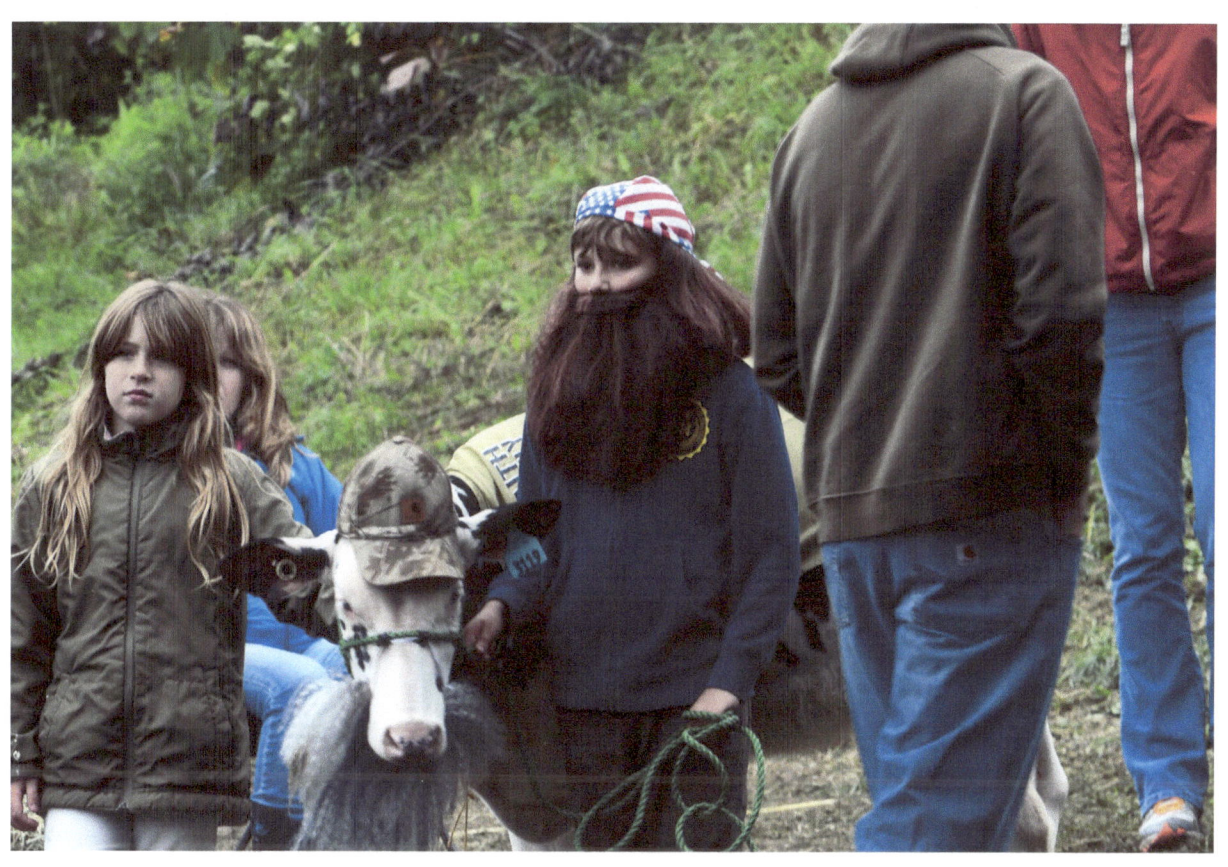

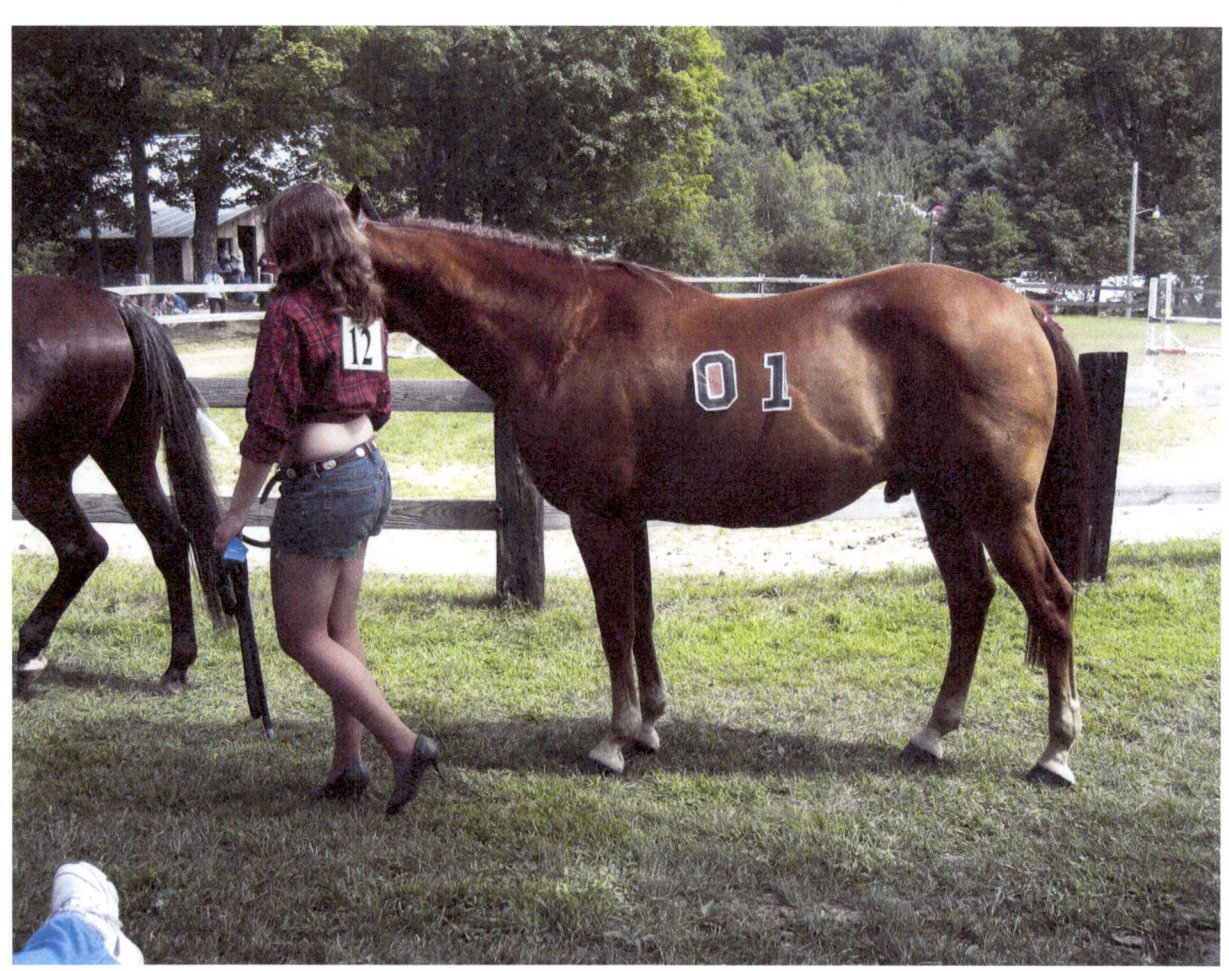

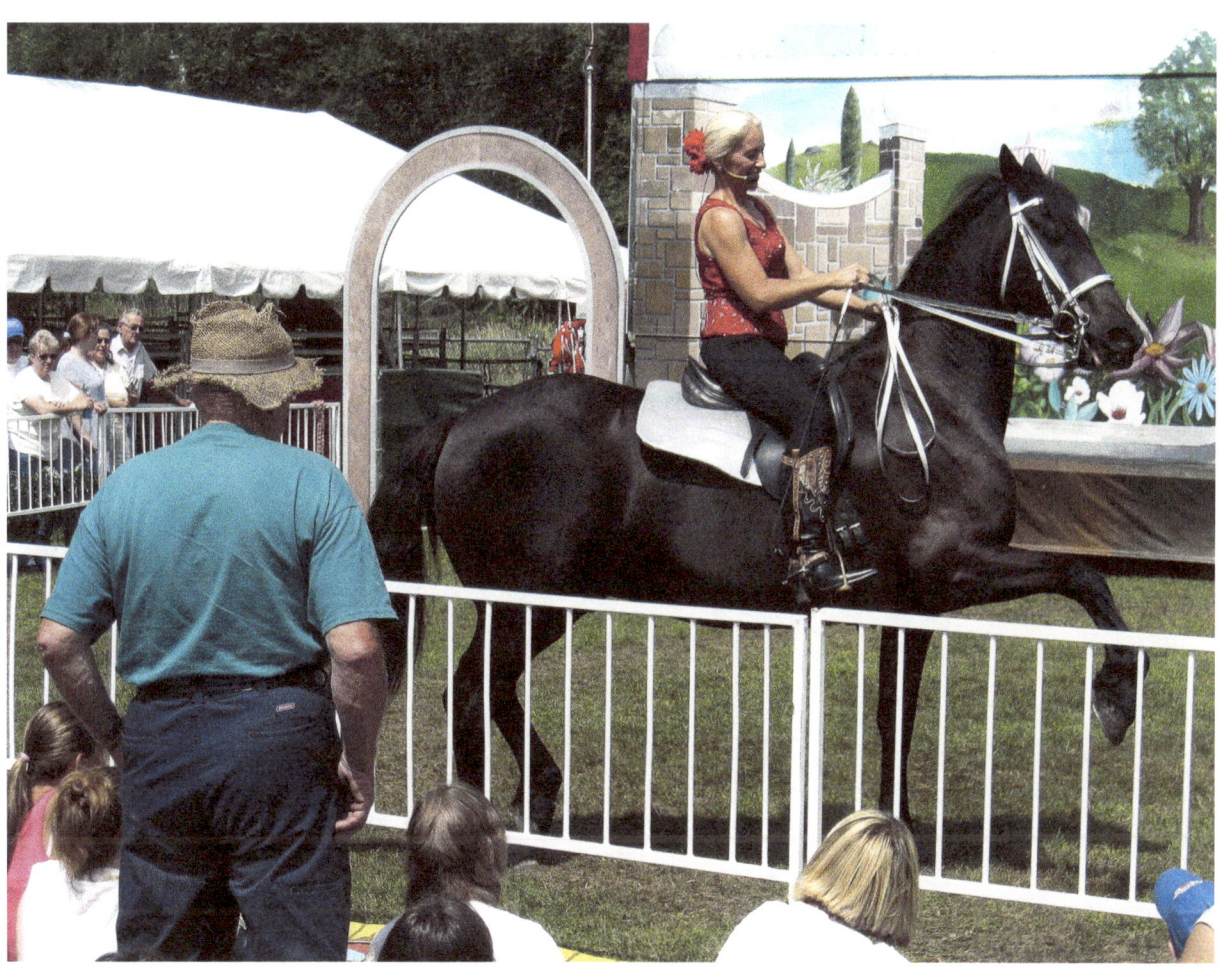

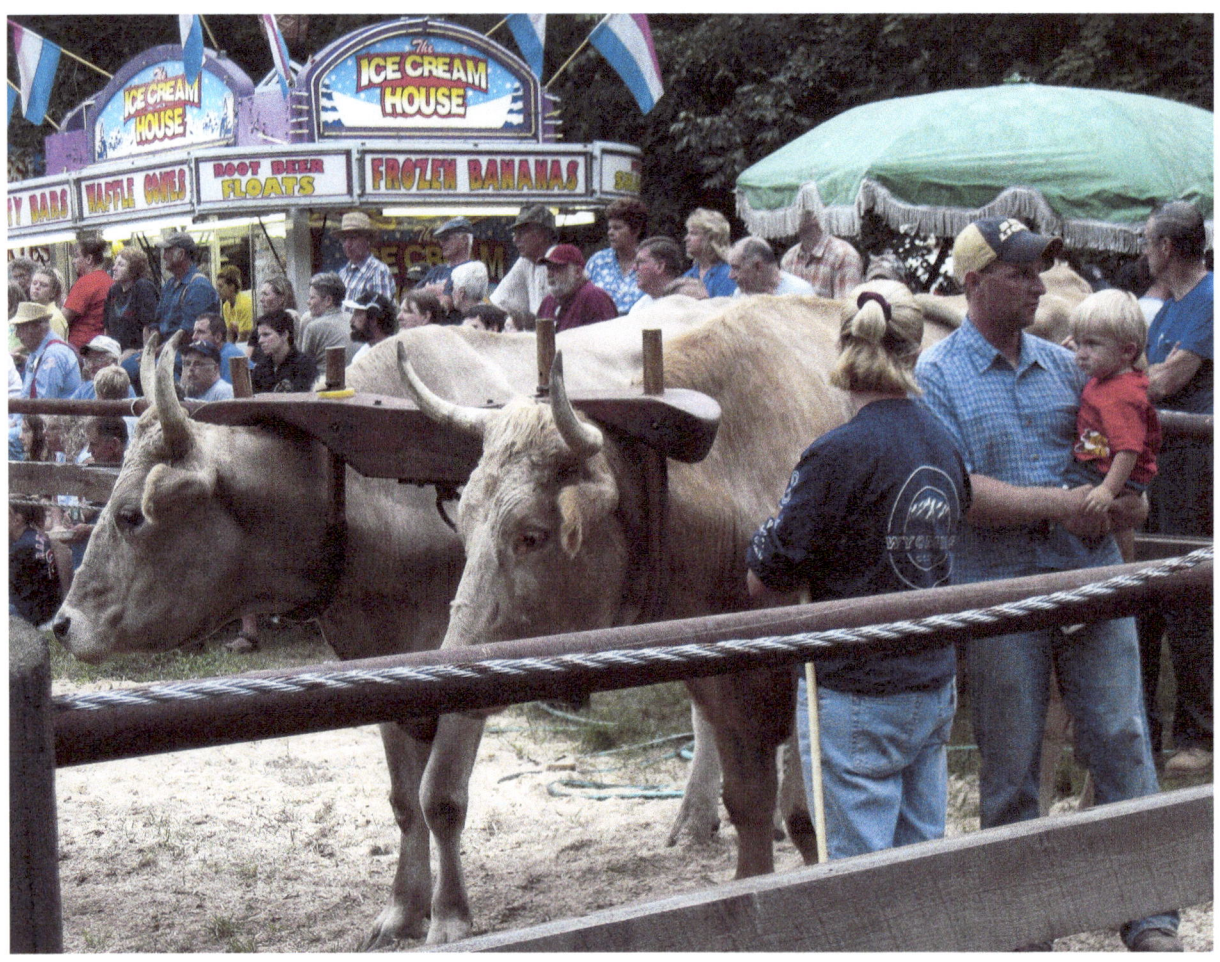

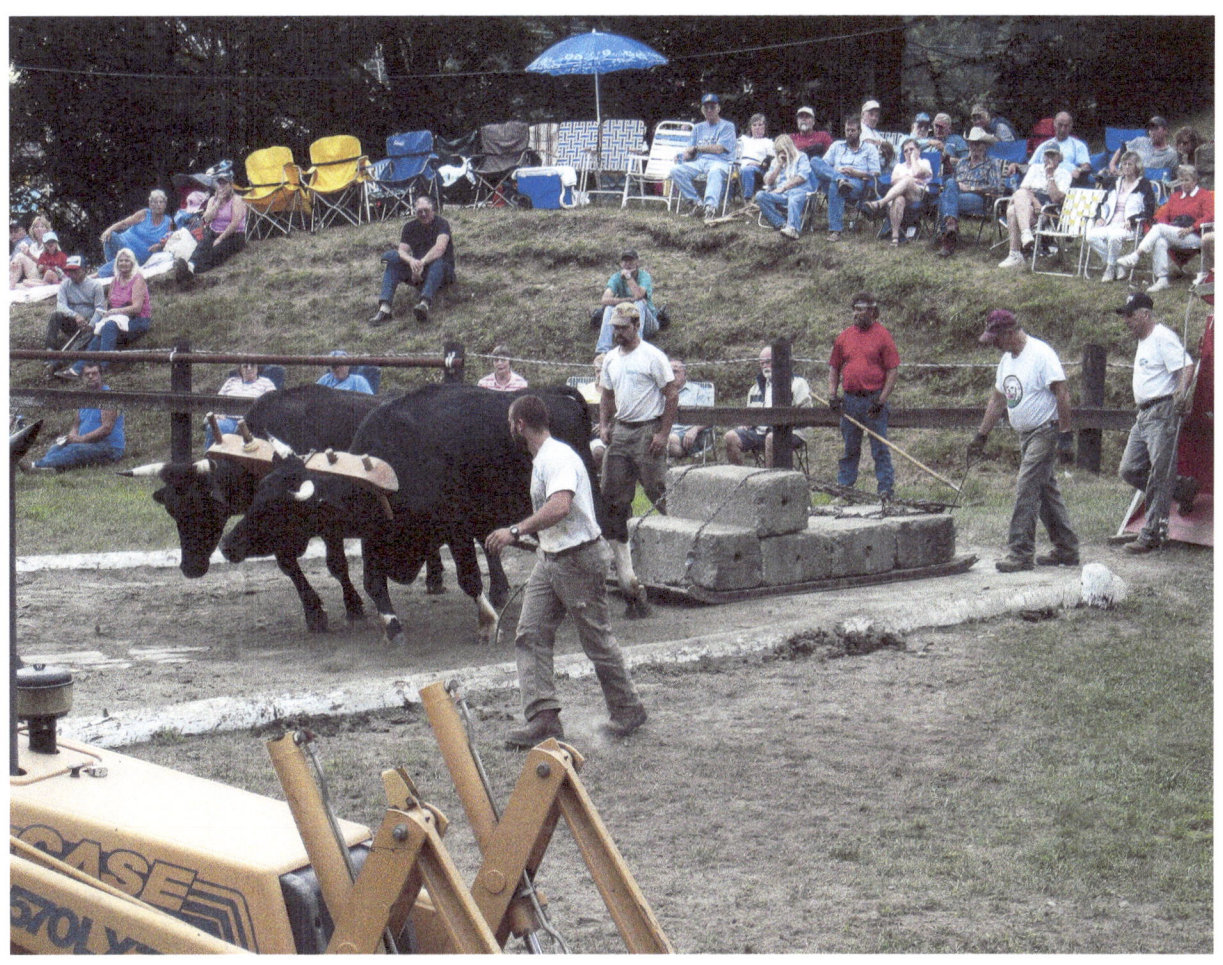

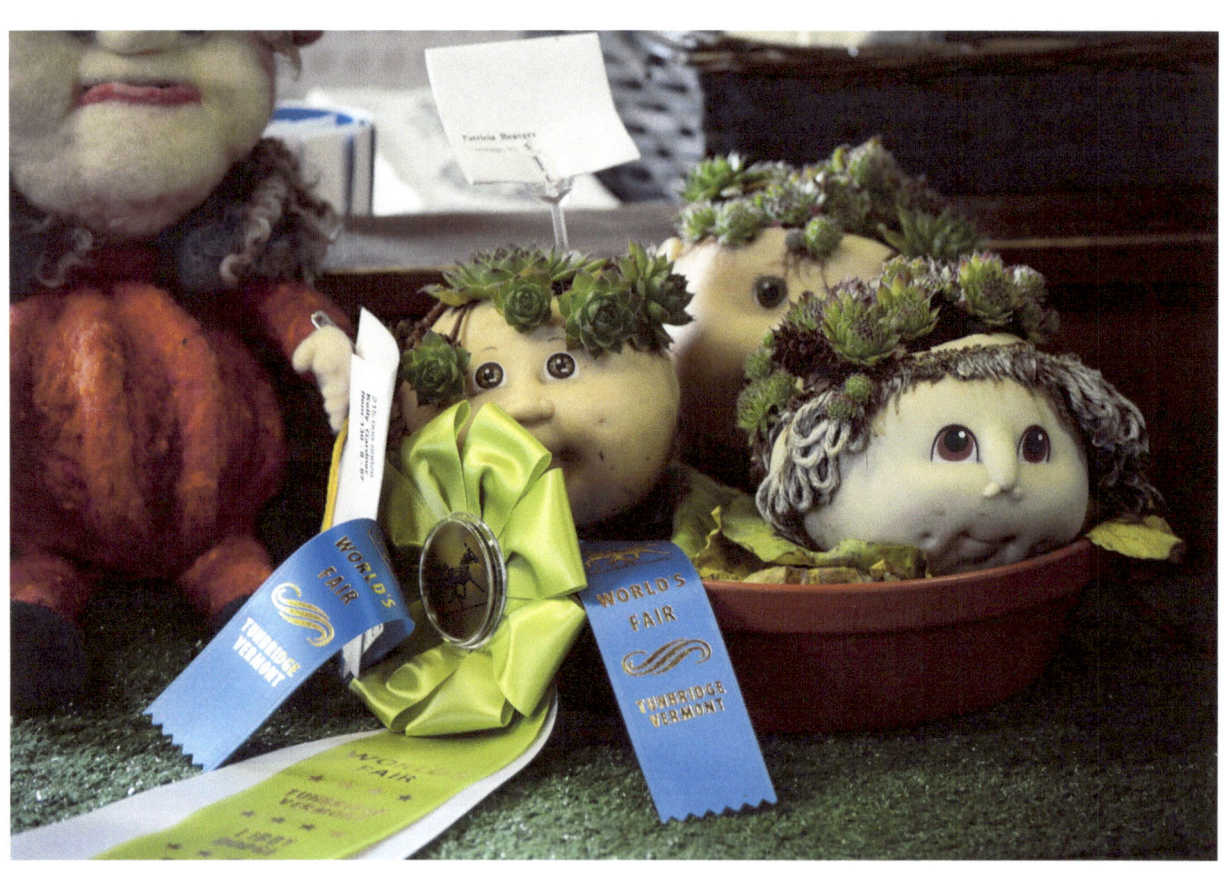

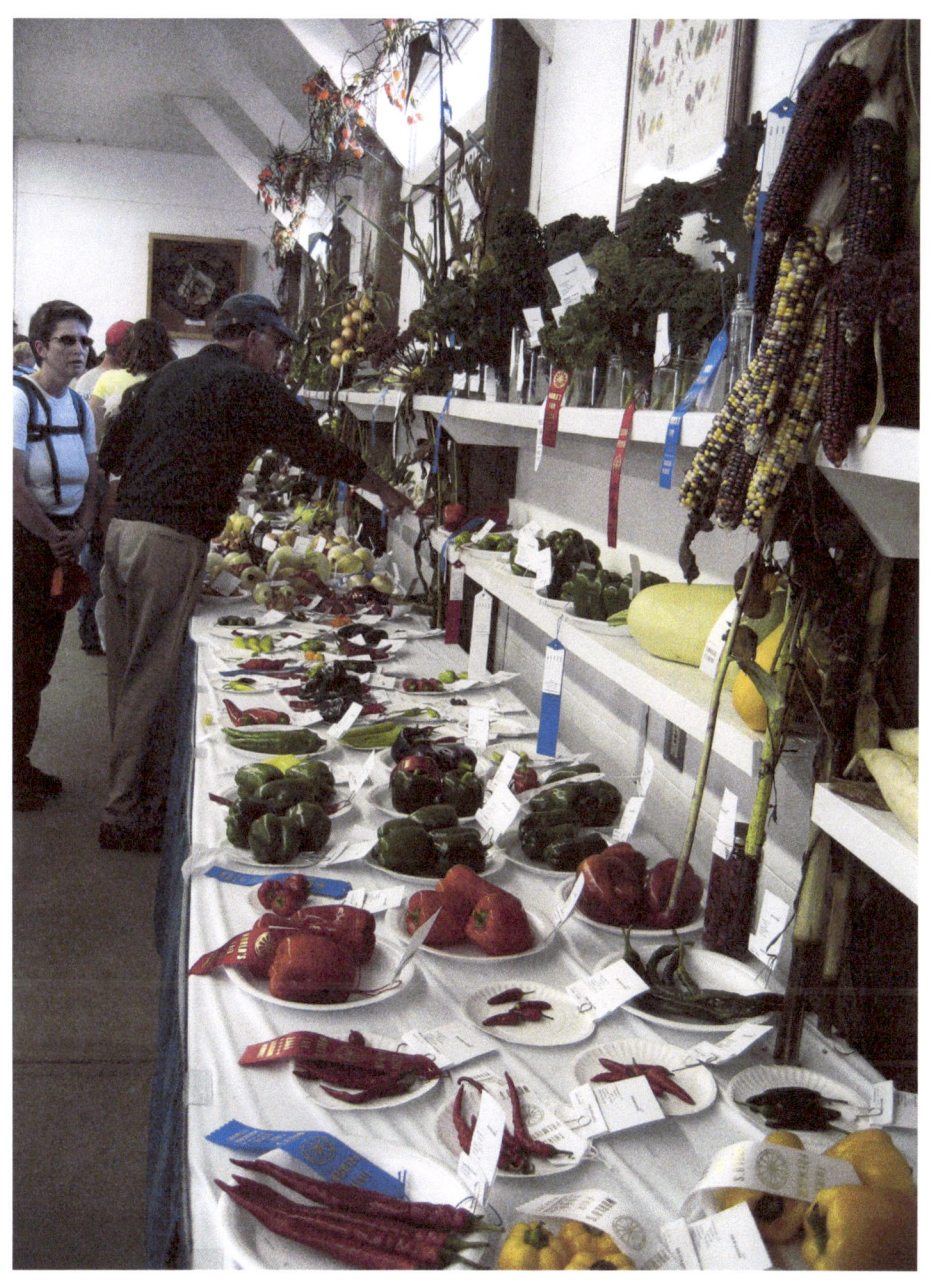

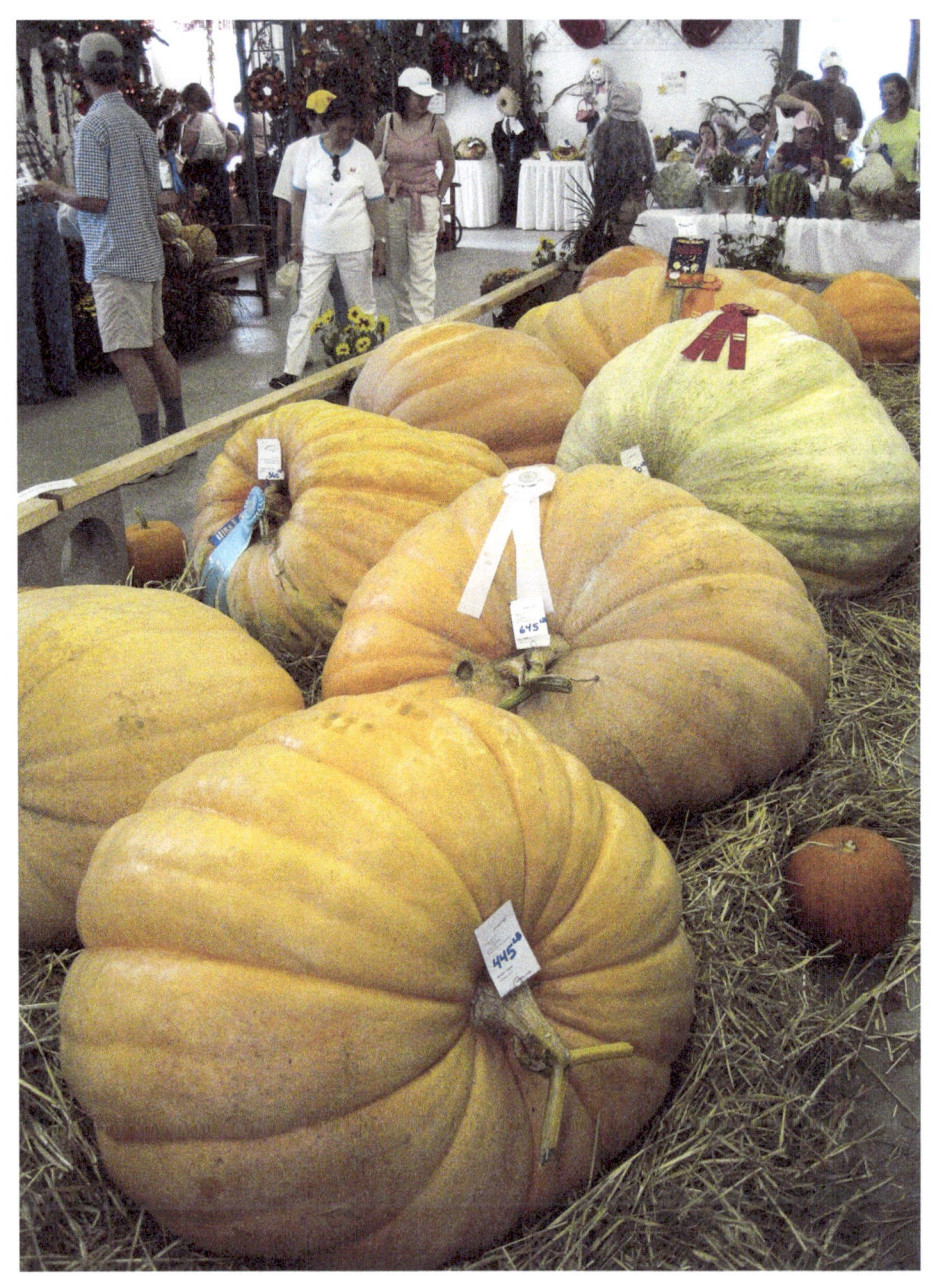

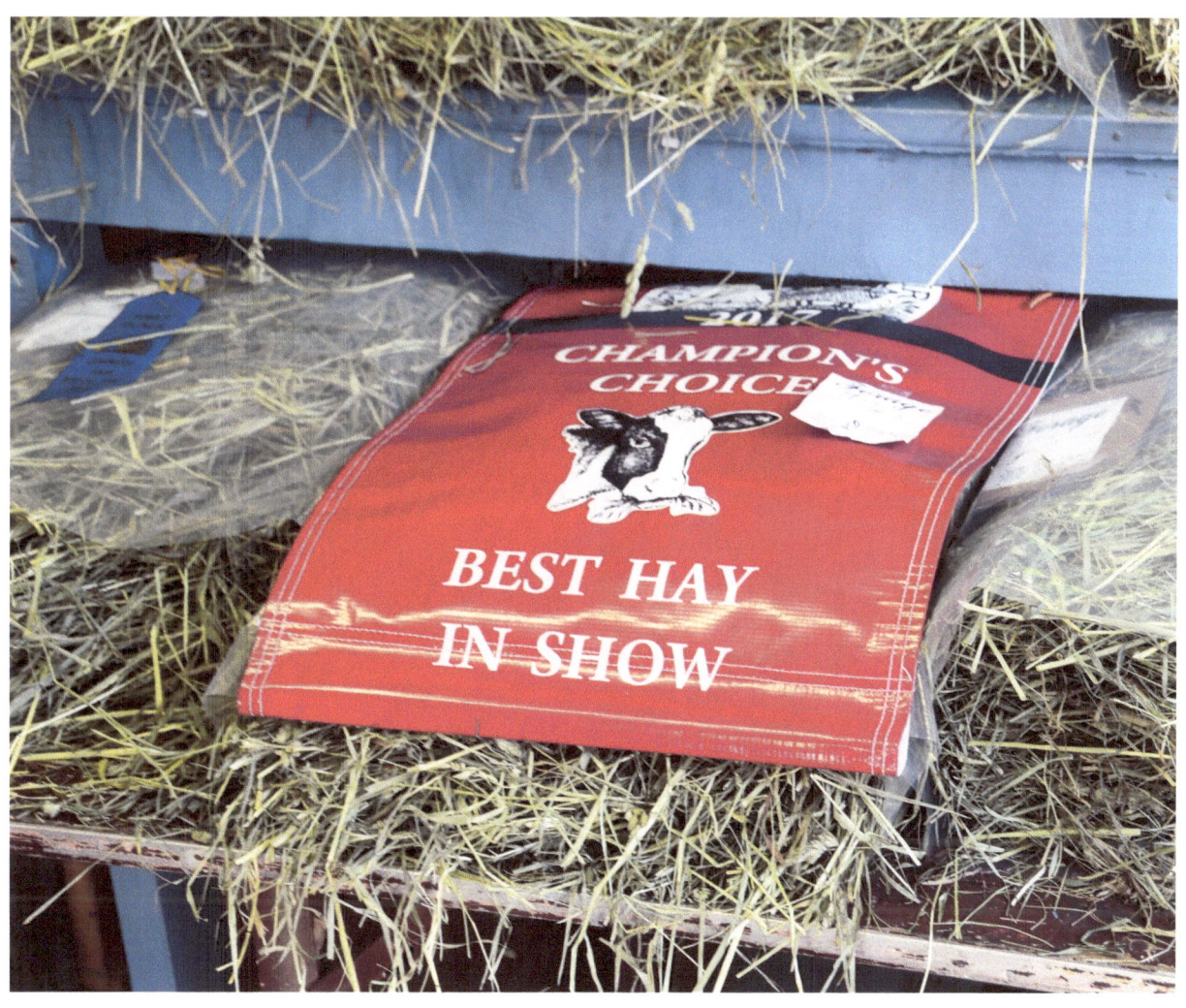

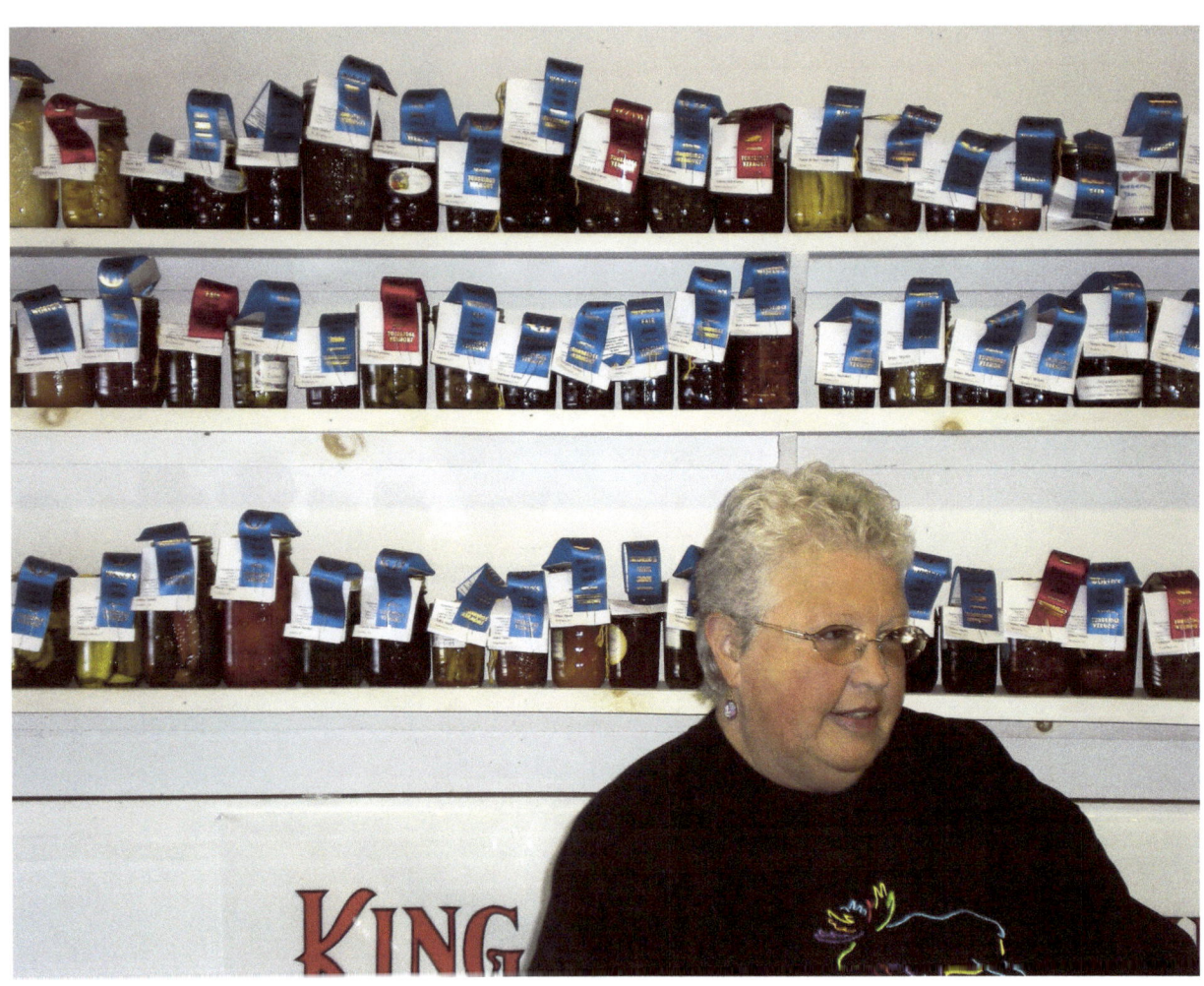

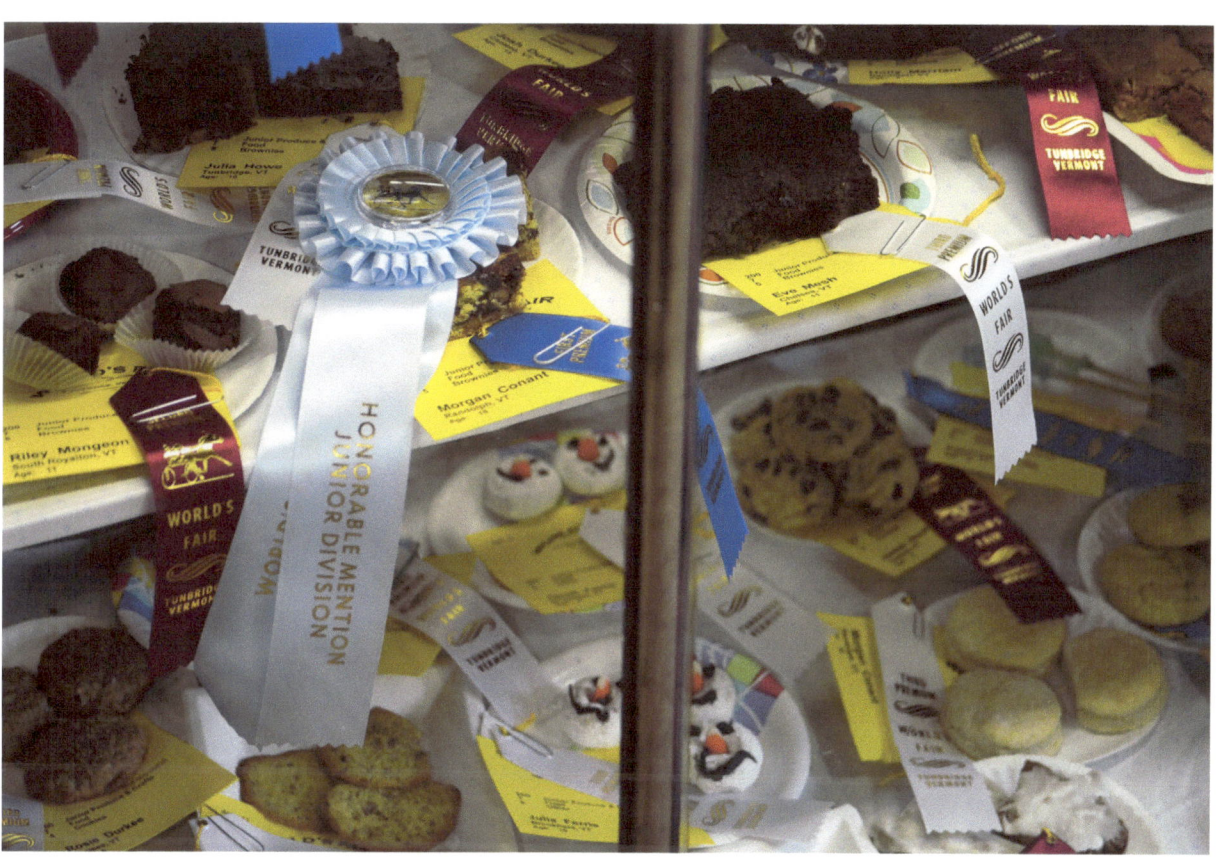

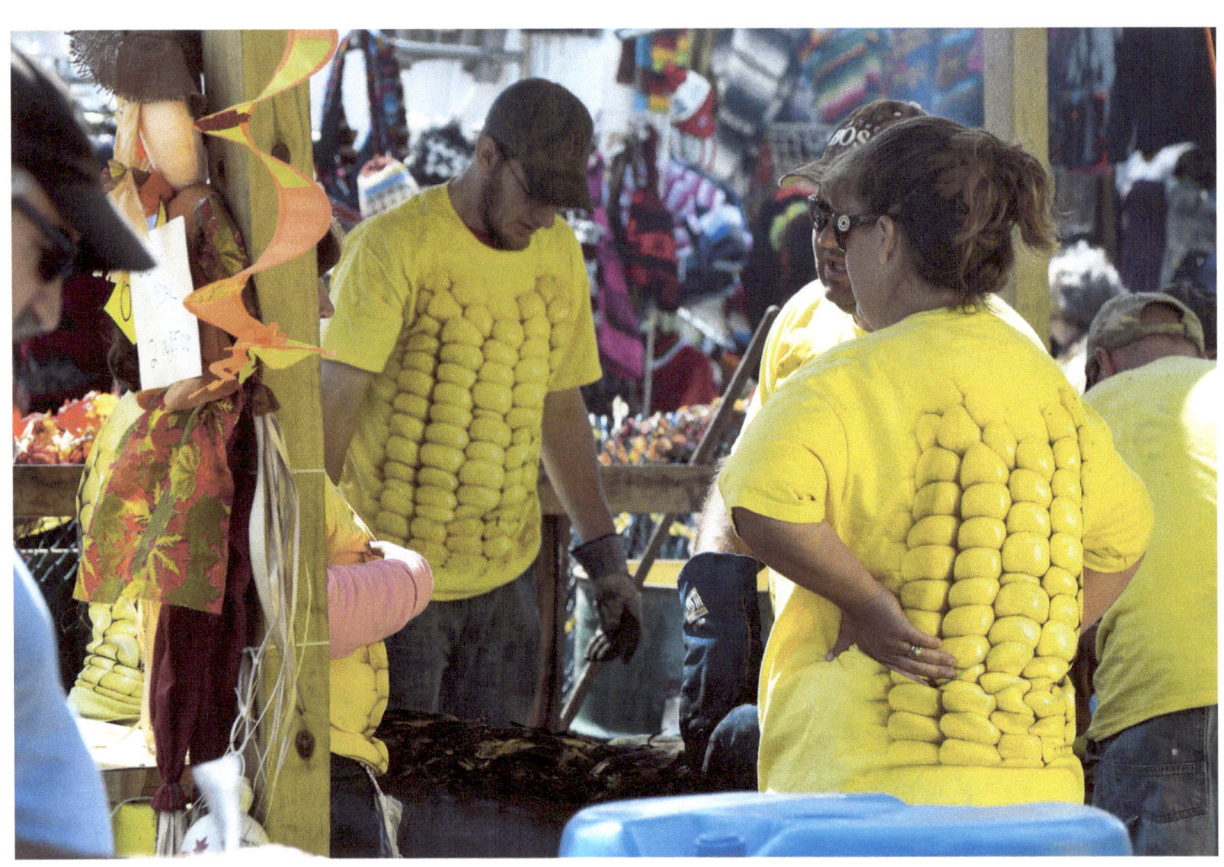

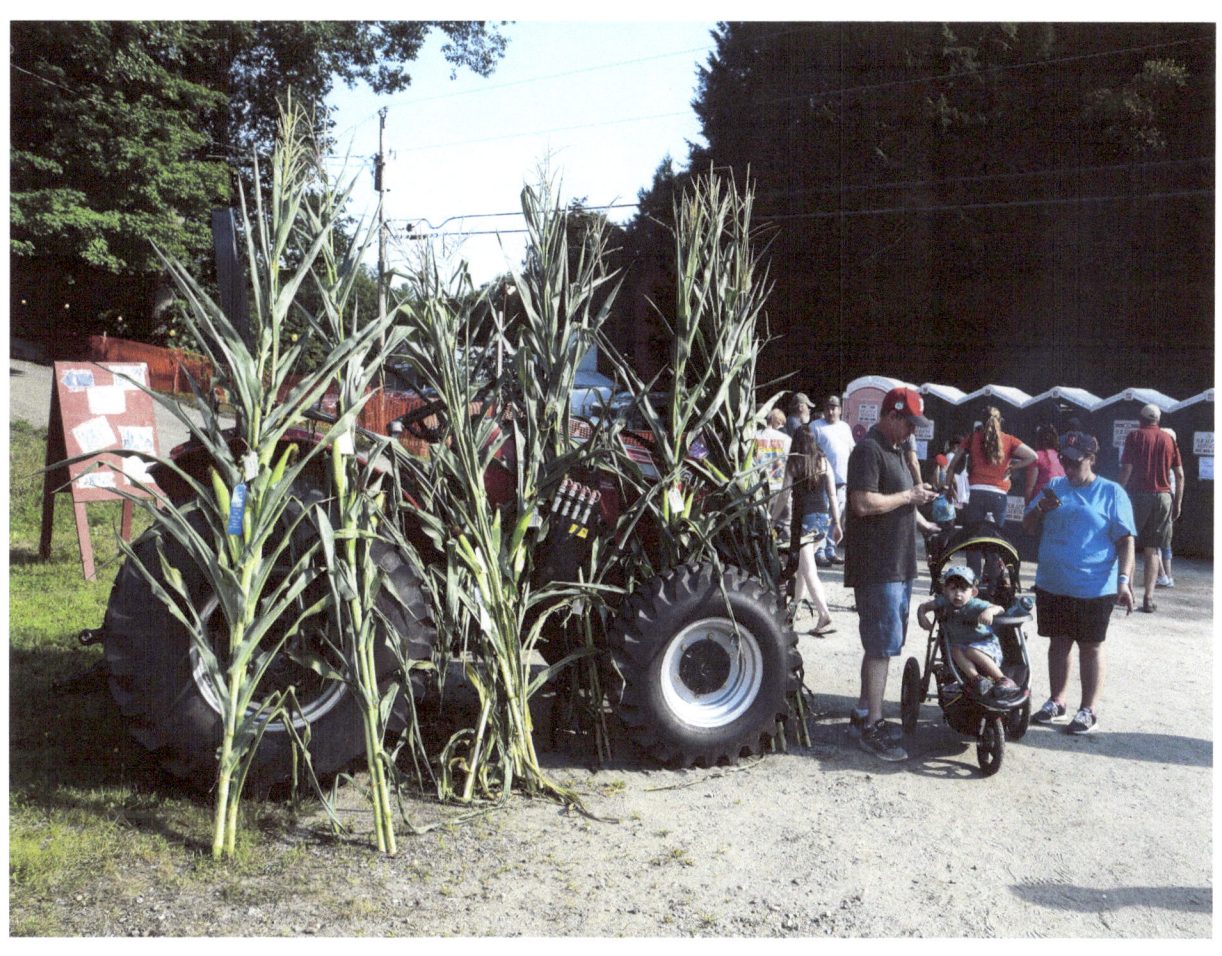

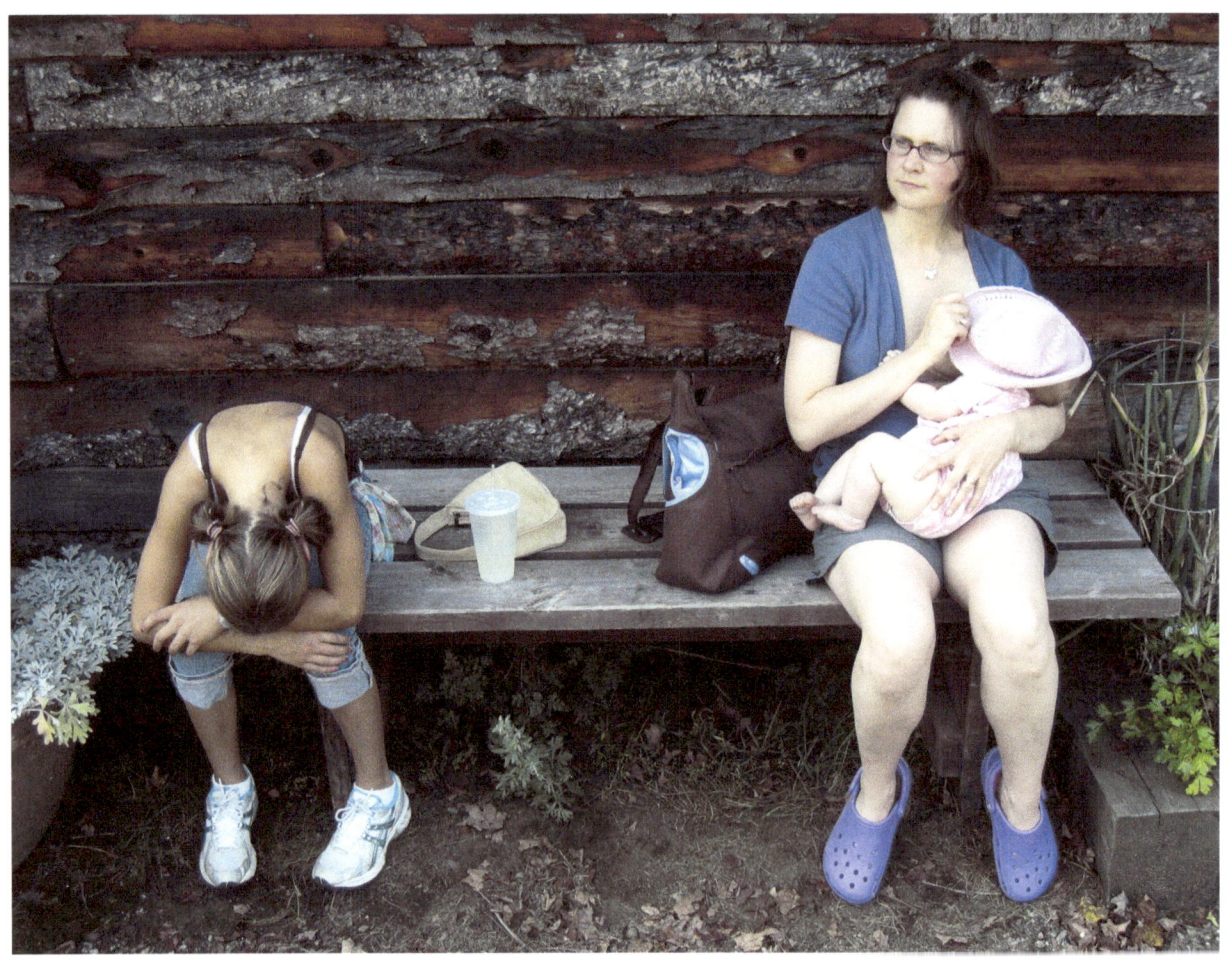

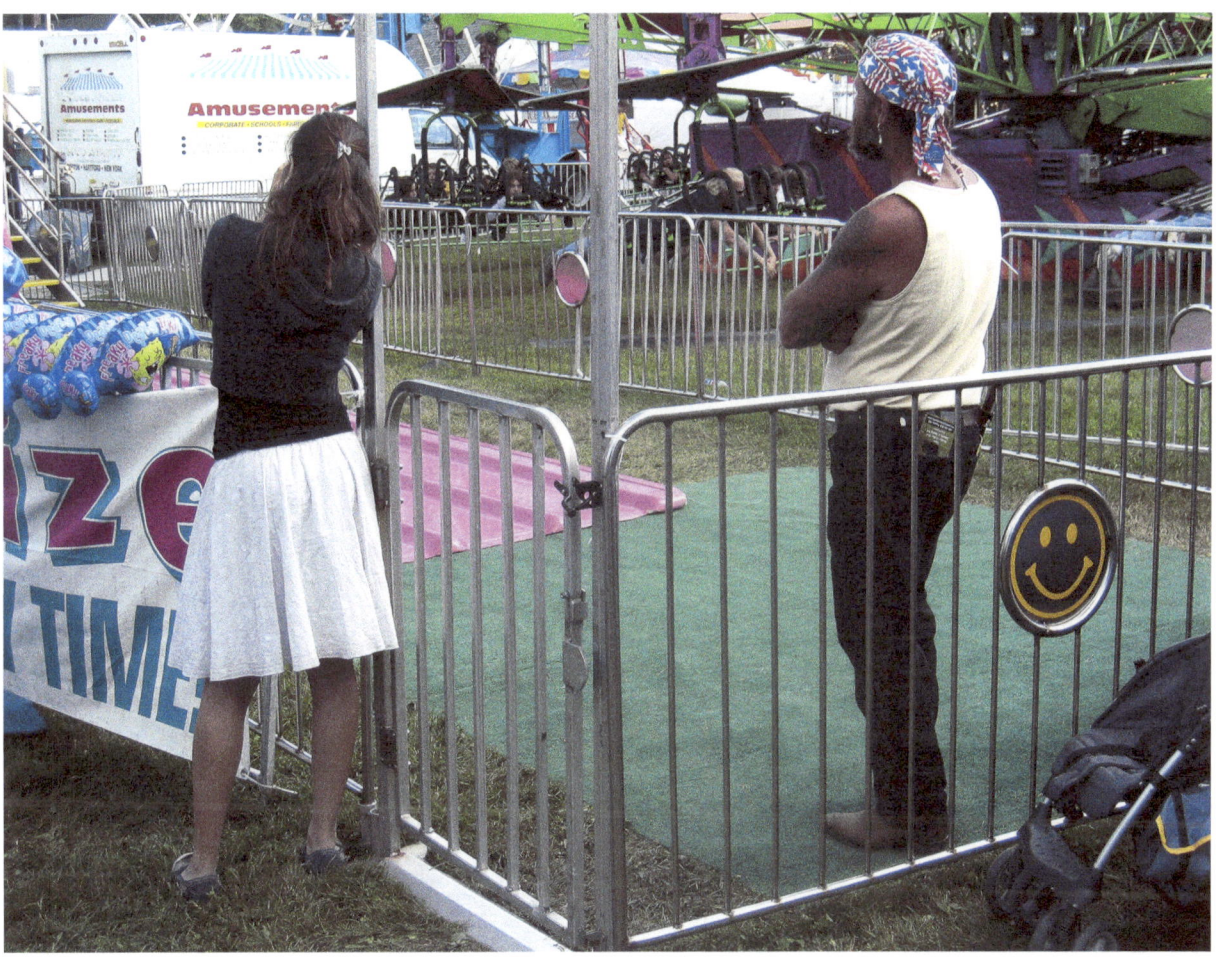

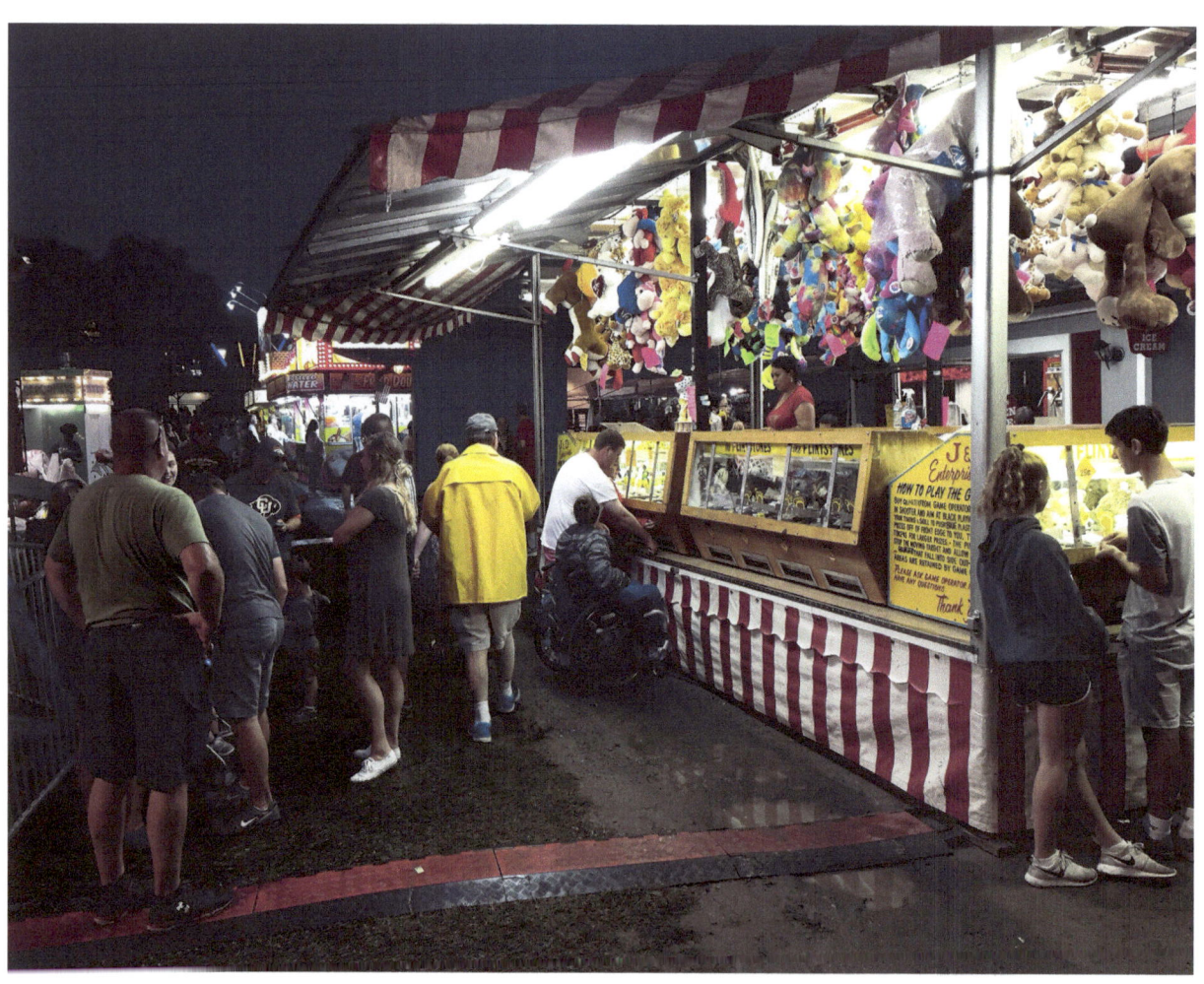

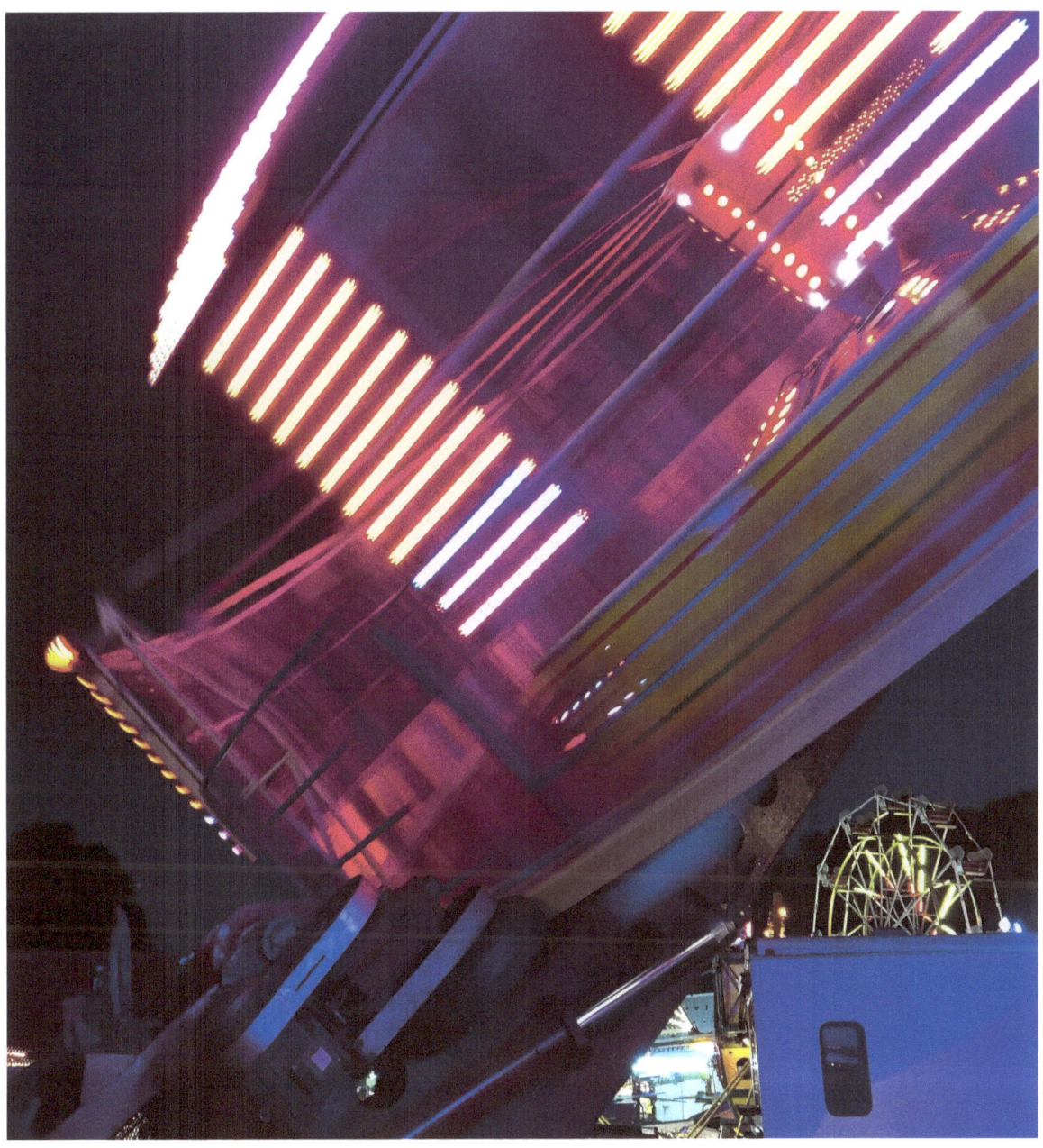

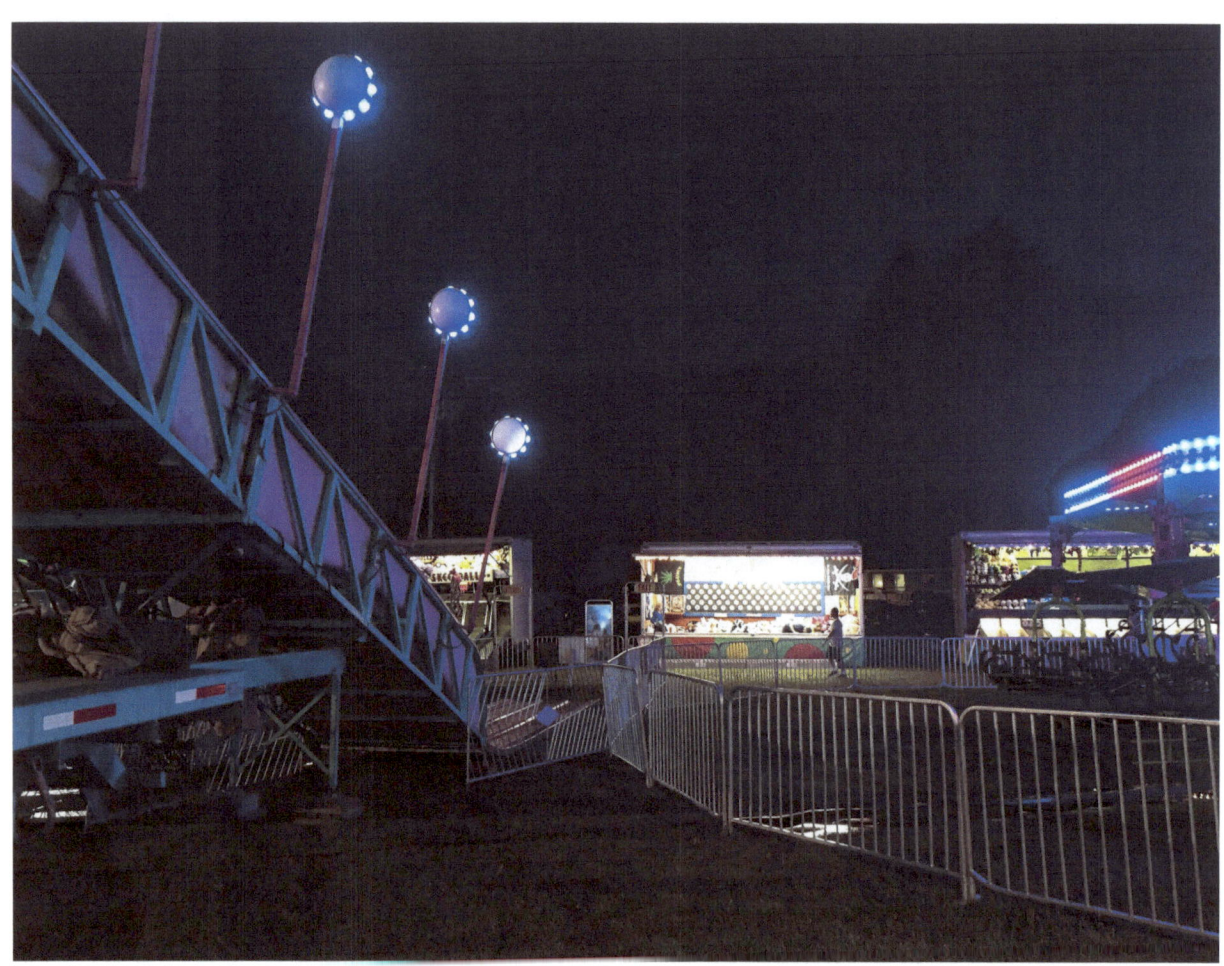

adamablue.com

www.ingramcontent.com/pod-product-compliance
Lightning Source LLC
Chambersburg PA
CBHW051204220526
45473CB00003B/893